INTRODUCTION OF THE CONSTITUTION OF THE REPUBLIC OF KOREA FOR FOREIGNERS' UNDERSTANDING

2025

Robert Rha

대한민국 헌법 영문판

초판인쇄	2025년 01월 18일
초판발행	2025년 01월 28일
편 저 자	Robert Rha
	(Mobile: 010 5848 7594 / E-mail: rha.robert@gmail.com)
발 행 인	韓 仁 培
펴 낸 곳	도서출판 북포럼, Bookorean
주 소	04559 서울시 중구 마른내로12길 7-4, 1002호(SOUTH KOREA)
전 화	010 6537 6869
팩 스	02 2277 6869
E-mail	938437@naver.com
등 록	725-09-02963
I S B N	979-11-989342-2-2, 13360
정가 Price	USA: US $ 9.90 / 대한민국: 10,000원(KRW)

- 이 책의 저작권은 책 저자에게 있으므로 무단 전재 및 복제를 금합니다.
   이 책을 무단 전재 또는 복제하면 「저작권법」 제136조에 의거 처벌을 받습니다.
- 도서출판 북포럼(한글명), Bookorean(영문명) 등록 완료.
- 파본은 구입하신 서점에서 교환하여 드립니다.

Contents

Introduction ··· 5

1. The Constitution of the Republic of Korea in English ············· 6

2. The Constitution of the Republic of Korea in Korean ············ 42
   (대한민국 헌법)

3. The Constitution of the United States ································ 62

4. The Constitution of the United States in Korean ················· 83
   (미합중국 헌법)

Introduction

The Republic of Korea has a democratic constitution like other independent countries worldwide. Since July 1948, the constitution has been amended nine times until now. This is the ninth amendment of the constitution. I would like to introduce foreign politicians, business persons, and students to the Korean constitution, which I have translated into English, for the fundamental understanding of the character of the Korean constitution including the distribution of power, acts and regulations, checks and balances, promotion of industrial development policies, the social environment of Korea, etc.

This may not be perfect for satisfying various demands or requirements from the Korean people concerning most free-living standards, less state interference in privacy, government obligations for the people, political institutions for people's participation, etc. The Korean constitution, however, has been established for the people of a democratic society, not for any socialists, absolutists, autocracies, or dictators, because democracy is the most efficient humanitarian political system in our human history.

As advanced Western democratic countries with liberty-originated legal systems for a long time, the Korean constitution would be amended continuously in the optimal direction as well, which could make Korean people keep living up to their free and safe personal standards, with justice and equal opportunity for all generations. I hope the current Constitution of the Republic of Korea can help you to understand more about Korean institutions, political systems, legal procedures, culture, society, etc.

Robert Rha

Copyright ©,2022 by Robert Rha.
By Korea Copyright Commission. All rights reserved. No part of this publication may be reproduced, stored in a retrieval system, or transmitted, in any form or by any means, otherwise, without the prior written permission of Robert Rha
Email: rha.robert@gmail.com

The Constitution of the Republic of Korea

Tenth Constitution
Ninth Amendment / Entire Amendment on October 29, 1987
Date of Enforcement: February 25, 1988

PREAMBLE

We, the people of Korea, being proud of a long and splendid history, are succeeding the legislation of the Provisional Republic of Korea Government, established after the March First Independence Movement on March 1, 1919, and the democratic ideology of the April Nineteenth Democratic Revolution on April 19, 1960. We keep on consolidating the national unity with justice, humanity, and fraternity based on the duty of democratic reformation and peaceful unification of the Korean peninsula; demolishing any social harmful habit and injustice; conforming to a free and democratic fundamental order based on autonomy and harmony; providing equal opportunity, to each individual, in any sectors concerning politics, economics, society and culture, and promoting the best ability of individuals; planning of equal development of livelihood of all people inward and contributing for permanent world peace and common prosperity of humankind outward, and; swearing to secure the permanent secure, freedom and happiness of ourselves and our descendants. We, hereby, amend the Constitution, which was established on July 12, 1948, amended eight times thereafter, by ratification from the National Assembly and a national referendum.

CHAPTER 1. GENERAL PROVISIONS

Article 1

(1) The Republic of Korea shall be a democratic republic.
(2) The sovereignty of the Republic of Korea shall be vested in the people; all power is derived from the people.

Article 2

(1) Nationality of the Republic of Korea shall be prescribed by acts.

(2) It shall be the liability of the State for protecting Korean people, residing out of the country, as prescribed by acts.

Article 3

The territory of the Republic of Korea shall consist of the Korean peninsula and insular areas belonging to the Republic of Korea.

Article 4

The Republic of Korea shall direct the peaceful unification of the Korean peninsula, and precede the establishment of a peaceful unification policy based on free and democratic fundamental order.

Article 5

(1) The Republic of Korea shall attempt to maintain international peace and repudiate any wars of aggression.

(2) The Armed Forces shall execute their mission, as the sacred duty for the national security and territory defense, and their political neutrality shall be observed.

Article 6

(1) Treaties, concluded and proclaimed by the Constitution and generally approved international laws and regulations, shall have the same effect as those of the Republic of Korea.

(2) The status of aliens shall be guaranteed according to the prescription of international laws and treaties.

Article 7

(1) Public officials shall be servants to all people and have the obligation to their service to the people.

(2) The status and political neutrality of public officials shall be guaranteed

as prescribed by acts.

Article 8

(1) People shall have the right to establish any political parties freely; the plural party system shall be guaranteed.
(2) Political parties shall be democratic in their objectives, organization, and activities, and shall have the necessary organization for participating in any form of political opinion from people.
(3) Political parties shall enjoy protection from the State; the State may provide political parties with required funds for party operation as prescribed by acts.
(4) If the purposes or activities of any political party are contrary to the fundamental democratic order, the Government may sue such parties for dissolution, and the ruling of the Constitutional Court shall dissolve the related parties.

Article 9

The State shall endeavor to succeed, promote the traditional culture, and enhance national culture.

CHAPTER 2. RIGHTS AND DUTIES OF PEOPLE

Article 10

All people shall enjoy dignity and worth as human beings, and have the right to pursue happiness. The State shall have an obligation to confirm and guarantee the fundamental human right of individuals not be infringed

Article 11

(1) All people are equal under the law. No people shall be discriminated against by sex, religion, or social status in any scope of political, economic, or cultural living

(2) No privileged social status or ranks shall be admitted; nor shall any establishment thereon be in whatever formation.

(3) Any honor or promotion from awarding medals, decorations, etc., shall be effective only for the related people, and no privilege shall be given thereto.

Article 12

(1) All people shall have the freedom of the body. All people shall not, except by acts thereof, be under arrest, restraint, search, or interrogation, or, except being through the due process of law thereof, not be under punishment, security confinement, or forced labor.

(2) All people shall not be under torture; nor shall be forced to state against their interest in being involved in any criminal cases.

(3) A warrant, issued by a judge upon the request by a prosecutor with the due process of law thereof, shall be presented to the related people, at the time of arrest, restraint, search, or seizure; however, in case of a suspected criminal in the very act of committing the crime, or apprehension of escape or destroying evidence by a suspected, who commits a crime to be the verdict of no less than three years, the post-warrant may be requested by a prosecutor after execution hereof.

(4) Any people shall have the right to receive counsel from an attorney, at the time of being under arrest or restraint; however, in case any criminal suspect cannot afford to have any assistance from an attorney, the State shall provide a public defender for the suspect thereof, as prescribed by acts.

(5) Any people shall not be under arrest or detention, without being notified of the reason for being under arrest or detention, and have the right to receive counsel from an attorney. The reason, date, and place regarding arrest or detention thereof shall be notified, without being delayed, to the related family members, etc., of legally designated.

(6) Any person shall have the right to request a review of the legality of arrest and detention to the court in case of being under arrest or detention.

(7) In case any confession from a defendant is recognized as not stated by free will, but by assault, threat, restraint, or unjustified long-term torture, deception, or other methods, or that the confession is the only evidence against a related defendant in any judicial hearing, the evidence thereof shall not be the proof for a verdict of guilty; neither shall be punished based on the proof thereon.

Article 13

(1) Any people shall not be prosecuted by any act, which is not prescribed as a crime by acts, at the time of committing the act thereof; nor shall be prosecuted or punished for the identical offense by double jeopardy.
(2) Any people shall not be, by any retroactive acts, under a restriction of the right for political participation, or not be deprived of proprietary right.
(3) Any people shall not be treated against their interest for any wrongdoing by their relatives, not by their wrongdoing.

Article 14

All people shall have the freedom of residence and migration.

Article 15

All people have the freedom to select their occupations.

Article 16

No people shall be infringed on the freedom of residence; for the execution of confiscation or search upon the residence, any warrant issued by a judge thereon, upon the request of a prosecutor, shall be presented to at the time of the execution.

Article 17

No people shall be fringed on the secret and freedom of privacy.

Article 18

No people shall be fringed on the secret of correspondence.

Article 19

All people shall enjoy the freedom of conscience.

Article 20

(1) All people shall enjoy the freedom of religion.
(2) No state religion shall be admitted; religions and politics shall be separated.

Article 21

(1) All people shall enjoy the freedom of the press, publication, assembly, and association.
(2) No permission or inspection for the press or publication shall be admitted; no permission for assembly and association shall be admitted.
(3) Any requirements necessary for the facility standards for communications and broadcastings and the guarantee of the function of newspapers shall be prescribed by acts.
(4) Neither press nor publication shall infringe on the honors or rights of any people, nor public morals and social ethics; in case of being infringed on honor or right by presses or publications, the related infringed ones may claim for the compensation thereon.

Article 22

(1) All people shall enjoy the freedom of learning and arts.
(2) The rights that belong to authors, inventors, scientists, technologists, and artists shall be protected by acts.

Article 23

(1) Property rights of all people shall be guaranteed. The contents and limitations thereof shall be prescribed by acts.

(2) The exercise of property rights shall be appropriate to the public welfare.

(3) Any eminent domain, use, or limitation of private property for a public purpose by the government shall be prescribed by acts, and the just compensation thereon shall be provided.

Article 24

All people shall have the right to vote as prescribed by acts.

Article 25

All people shall have the political rights of holding public office as prescribed by acts.

Article 26

(1) All people shall have the right to file written petitions with any agencies in the State as prescribed by acts.

(2) The state shall have obligations to examine the written petitions thereof.

Article 27

(1) All people shall have the right to a judicial trial in courts by related judges prescribed by the Constitution and acts, with due process of law.

(2) All people, except those being status of military service or civilian employees for military forces, shall not have judicial trials in military courts, within the territory of the Republic of Korea, unless committing any crime prescribed by acts related to critical military secrets, sentries, sentry boxes, or providing poisoned foods or beverages, or being prisoners of war or articles for military purpose, or in case of being under a declaration of the extraordinary martial law.

(3) All people shall have the right to an immediate trial. Any people, accused of a criminal act, shall have the right to a public trial without delay unless the accused has an adequate reason for being delayed.

(4) Any people charged with a criminal offense shall have the right to be

presumed innocent until proven guilty.

(5) Any crime victims may make statements in the process of trials thereon as prescribed by acts.

Article 28

In case any criminal suspect or defendant in custody is judged not indicted, or sentenced to acquittal, as prescribed by acts, the related people shall be entitled to claim just compensation from the State, as the prescription by acts.

Article 29

(1) Any people, damaged due to unlawful action by public officials on duties, shall have the right to claim just compensation from the State or public organization, as prescribed by acts; in this case, public officials, being concerned thereon, shall not be exempted from the obligation.

(2) Any people, under the status of military service, or a civilian employee for military forces, or a police officer, or any ones, prescribed by acts, shall not claim any compensation from the State or public organizations, in case of committing unlawful actions on duties, related to the execution of duties of combats or drills, etc., except compensations prescribed by acts.

Article 30

Any people, inflicted on life or body by criminal offenses of others, may receive rescue regarding the infliction from the State, as prescribed by acts.

Article 31

(1) All people have the right to have equal education upon their ability.
(2) All people shall have the obligation to provide their children, under their care, with the elementary education course, at least, and other education courses as prescribed by acts.
(3) The compulsory education shall be free from the education fees.
(4) The independence, specialty, and political impartiality of the education

and the autonomy of colleges or universities shall be guaranteed as prescribed by acts.

(5) The State shall promote lifelong education for the people.

(6) The fundamental requirements for the education system, including education in school and lifelong education, education management, education finances and the status of educators shall be as prescribed by acts.

Article 32

(1) All people have labor rights. The State shall endeavor to, with social and economic policies, promote the employment of laborers, guarantee moderate wages, and execute the minimum wage system as prescribed by acts.

(2) All people shall have the duty of labor. The State shall prescribe, according to the democratic principles, the contents, and conditions of duty for labor by acts.

(3) Standards for labor conditions shall be prescribed by acts to secure human dignity.

(4) The labor of women shall be under special protection, and shall not be subject to unjust discrimination in employment, wages, and working conditions.

(5) The labor of minors shall be under special protection.

(6) Any surviving family of State heroes for public services; of dead or wounded soldiers in action; of died or wounded police officers in action shall be entitled to priority of the labor opportunity.

Article 33

(1) Workers shall have the right to independent association, collective bargaining, and collective action for the improvement of the working conditions.

(2) Limited workers prescribed by acts, as public officers of government agencies, shall have the right to collective association, collective bargaining, and collective action.

designated by acts may be restricted or denied as prescribed by acts.

(3) The right to the collective action of workers, who work for the major State defense industries designated by acts, may be restricted or denied as prescribed by acts.

Article 34

(1) All people shall have the right to live in worth as human beings.
(2) The State shall have the obligation to make an effort to promote social security and the social welfare of the people.
(3) The State shall make an effort to promote the welfare and rights of women.
(4) The State shall have the obligation to execute the policies to promote the welfare of seniors and adolescents.
(5) Any people, being unable to make a living due to a disabled body, disease or old age shall be protected by the State as prescribed by acts.
(6) The State shall make an effort to prevent all people from any disaster and protect them against hazards thereon.

Article 35

(1) All people shall have the right to live in a healthy and comfortable environment, and the State and people both shall make an effort to keep the environment safe.
(2) Contents and execution of the environmental rights shall be prescribed by acts.
(3) The state shall make an effort to enable all people to enjoy comfortable living with housing development policies, etc.

Article 36

(1) Establishment of marriage and family living shall be based on individual dignity and sexual equality, and be kept sustaining; the State shall secure thereon.
(2) The State shall make an effort to protect the maternal instinct and behavior.
(3) All people shall have the protection rights, by the State, related to their health.

Article 37

(1) Freedom and rights of all people shall not be neglected due to not being specified or listed in the Constitution.
(2) Freedom and rights may be restricted by acts, in case of being limited necessary for national security, keeping order, or public welfare; even in such case, the restriction shall not infringe on the essential contents of the freedom and rights.

Article 38

All people shall bear the tax liability as prescribed by acts.

Article 39

(1) All people shall bear the duty of national defense as prescribed by acts.
(2) Any people, who bear the duty of national defense with military service, shall not be at a disadvantage caused by bearing duties thereupon.

CHAPTER 3. THE NATIONAL ASSEMBLY

Article 40

The legislative power shall be vested in the National Assembly.

Article 41

(1) The National Assembly shall be composed of members, elected by vote of the people, according to universal, equal, direct, and secret suffrage election.
(2) The number of the National Assembly members shall be prescribed by acts; however, be not less than two hundred.
(3) The electoral districts, proportionally representing Assembly members and other requirements related to the election shall be prescribed by acts.

Article 42

The term of the National Assembly Members shall be for four years in office.

Article 43

Members of the National Assembly, at the same time, shall not hold any other office prescribed by acts.

Article 44

(1) Any members of the National Assembly, except in the case of being under a suspected criminal in the very act of committing the crime, shall be privileged from arrest or detention during their attendance at sessions of the National Assembly, without the consent of the National Assembly.

(2) In case of being arrested or detained before sessions of the National Assembly, any member of the National Assembly thereof, shall be released upon the request from the National Assembly, except being under a suspected criminal in the very act of committing the crime.

Article 45

Regarding any speeches or votes officially done in the National Assembly, any members of the National Assembly shall not be responsible for thereon outside the National Assembly.

Article 46

(1) Members of the National Assembly shall have the obligation to be uncorrupted.

(2) Members of the National Assembly shall hold their office, with the prior interest of the State interests, according to their conscience.

(3) Members of the National Assembly shall not take advantage of their status for acquiring any private rights or interests or any positions, by making contracts or achievements with the State, public organizations, or private enterprises; nor shall make any acquirements of achievements for others.

Article 47

(1) The National Assembly shall have the regular session one time every

year as prescribed by acts; and shall have the extraordinary sessions at the request of the President or of not less than one-fourth of enrolled members.

(2) The regular session of the National Assembly shall not exceed one hundred days; any extraordinary sessions shall not exceed thirty days respectively.

(3) The President shall specify the period and reasons for an extraordinary session at the time of requesting the National Assembly thereof.

Article 48

The National Assembly shall vote in one Speaker and two Vice-Speakers.

Article 49

The National Assembly, otherwise specified in the Constitution or any act, shall resolute any bill with the concurrence of a majority vote of members present, being in attendance of a majority of enrolled members. In case of being equal in number, the bill shall be regarded as rejected.

Article 50

(1) All sessions of the National Assembly shall be publicized; however, in case of concurrence of a majority present, or of being admitted by the Speaker for national security necessity, related sessions may not be publicized.

(2) Announcement of any contents, not being publicized, resulting from the consideration in the National Assembly, shall be as prescribed by acts.

Article 51

Any Bills or other proposals addressed for approval from the National Assembly shall not be abolished, on the ground of not being adopted during the related session; however, when the tenure of members of the National Assembly has expired, such Bills or proposals will be abolished.

Article 52

Any members of the National Assembly and the Government may have the right to address Bills to the National Assembly.

Article 53

(1) Any Bill passed in the National Assembly, shall be delivered to the Government, and the President shall promulgate within fifteen days.

(2) In case of having any objections to the delivered Bill, the President may return the delivered Bill with the documents expressing the reason for objection, within the period thereof Section (1) thereof, and require the returned Bill for reconsidering in the National Assembly; even in adjournment of session, the President may also require for reconsidering the Bill thereof.

(3) The President shall request neither any partial reconsidering nor modifying of the Bill returned to the National Assembly.

(4) In case of a request for reconsidering of the Bill, returned to the National Assembly from the President, the National Assembly shall address the Bill thereof for reconsidering; in case of concurrence of the two-thirds majority present, in attendance of a majority of the enrolled members in the National Assembly, the Bill thereof shall be passed, and be the Act.

(5) Even if the President will not promulgate the Act, or will not request reconsidering of the Bill, previously passed in the National Assembly, within the period thereof in Section (1) thereof, the Bill thereof shall be passed as being the Act.

(6) The President shall promulgate the Act, passed according to regulations in Section (4), (5) thereof, without delay. In case the President will not promulgate, within five days, the Act passed by Section (5) or the Act delivered to the Government after being passed by Section (4), the Speaker in the National Assembly shall promulgate the Act.

(7) Otherwise prescribed especially, the Act thereof shall validate after twenty days from the date of promulgation.

Article 54

(1) The National Assembly shall deliberate submitted proposals of National Budget Bills from the Government, and resolute the Bills.

(2) The Government shall plan budget Bills for every fiscal year and, thereafter, submit the planned Bills within ninety days before the beginning of each fiscal year; the National Assembly shall resolve each Bill within thirty days before the beginning of each fiscal year.

(3) In case of no result of each Bill before the beginning of the new fiscal year, the Government may execute, based on the budget of the last fiscal year, expenses for the following purposes, before the resolution of the National Assembly:

1. Expenses for the operation and management of official agencies and facilities established according to the Constitution or act
2. Expenses for the execution of obligatory expenditure prescribed by acts
3. Expenditure for the continuation of execution of any projects approved previously in the budget

Article 55

(1) In case of is necessary to continue the expenditure, to be more than one fiscal year, the Government shall obtain the resolution from the National Assembly related to the Continuation of Expenditure by specifying the period for execution.

(2) The Reserve Budget shall obtain the resolution from the National Assembly in total amount; any expenditure of the Reserve Budget shall require approval during the next secession of the National Assembly.

Article 56

In case of is necessary to modify any National Budget, the Government may submit the revised supplementary of the National Budget to the National Assembly for resolution.

Article 57

The National Assembly, without any consent from the Government, shall neither increase the expenditure upon any individual items in the Budget nor list any additional items in the budget submitted by the Government.

Article 58

The Government, except in cases of issuing national bonds or concluding any contracts, that may incur any burden, exceeding the Budget, to the State, shall obtain the resolutions from the National Assembly in advance.

Article 59

Classification, list, and rate of tax shall be prescribed by acts.

Article 60

(1) The National Assembly shall have the right to consent to conclusion and ratification related to any treaty for mutual assistance; treaty for security; treaty for important international organization; treaty for amity, commerce, and navigation; treaty for sovereignty restriction; treaty for peace; treaty regarding critical financial burdens on the State or people; treaty for initialization of Bills.

(2) The National Assembly shall have the right to consent to the declaration of war; dispatch of armed forces to foreign states; the station of foreign armed forces within the territory of the Republic of Korea.

Article 61

(1) The National Assembly may inspect any affairs of the State, or investigate any specific issues of the State; it may require the submission of necessary documents, the attendance of witnesses, the witness's testimony, or the witness's affidavit thereon.

(2) The procedure and other requirements for the inspection and investigation by the National Assembly shall be prescribed by acts.

Article 62

(1) The Prime Minister, Ministers of the State, or council members of the State may attend, report, state opinions or respond to inquiries regarding the administration procedure of the State in the National Assembly or at its committees.

(2) In case of being upon request by the National Assembly or its committees, the Prime Minister, Ministers of the State, or council members of the State shall attend the National Assembly and respond to inquiries; upon request for the attendance of the Prime Minister or Ministers of the State, Ministers of the State or Council Members of the State may attend and respond the inquiries.

Article 63

(1) The National Assembly may suggest that the President shall dismiss the Prime Minister or any Ministers from the respective office of the State.

(2) The suggestion of dismissal, according to Section (1) thereof, shall require a majority vote of enrolled members, regarding any proposal by no less than one-third of enrolled members,

Article 64

(1) The National Assembly may establish rules for the proceeding of the session and internal regulations within the scope of not violating the acts.

(2) The National Assembly may audit the qualification of its members, and punish its members.

(3) The National Assembly shall require the concurrence of a two-thirds majority of the enrolled members to expel any of its members.

(4) Any related members shall not sue in court regarding the expulsion due to the process according to Section (2) and (3) thereof.

Article 65

(1) In case of violation of the Constitution or acts during the execution of the respective official duty by the President, the Prime Minister,

members of the State Council, Ministers of the Administration, judges of the Constitutional Court of Korea, judges of the Court of Korea, council members of the National Election Commission, the Chairman and council members of the Board of Audit and Inspection of Korea, or other public officials prescribed by acts, the National Assembly may resolve the impeachment proceeding.

(2) The impeachment proceeding proposal, according to Section (1) thereof, shall require a proposal of no less than one-third of enrolled members of the National Assembly, and the resolution shall require the concurrence of a majority of the enrolled members; however, the impeachment proceeding proposal against the President shall require a proposal of majority of enrolled members of the National Assembly, and the resolution shall require the concurrence of a two-thirds majority of the enrolled members.

(3) Upon resolution of the impeachment proceeding procedure, the official execution right of any impeached officer shall be suspended until the day of the impeachment ruling.

(4) The impeachment ruling shall dismiss any impeached officer from the just public office itself; however, the ruling shall not exempt the related impeached officer from civil or criminal liability.

CHAPTER 4. GOVERNMENT

SECTION 1. The President

Article 66

(1) The President shall be the Head of State and represent the State in the relations with foreign states.

(2) The President shall have the responsibility and obligation for national independence, territory preservation, national continuity, and protection of the Constitution.

(3) The President shall have the faithful obligation for the peaceful unification

of the homeland.

(4) The right to Administration shall be vested in the Government headed by the President.

Article 67

(1) The President shall be elected by universal, equal, direct, and secret ballot by the people.

(2) In case of being resulted in no less than two candidates with equal highest votes in the presidential election, according to Section (1) thereof, the National Assembly shall determine the President by the concurrence of a majority vote in attendance of a majority of enrolled members.

(3) In case of being resulted in one presidential candidate registered for the election, the sole candidate shall never be elected the President without acquiring a one-third majority of the total voters in the Presidential Election.

(4) Any candidates for the Presidency shall reach the age of forty years at the time of Election Day with the right to be elected for being a member of the National Assembly.

(5) Requirements for the Presidential election shall be prescribed by acts.

Article 68

(1) The President for the next term shall be elected within seventy to forty days before the termination of office term of the incumbent President.

(2) In case of becoming vacant of the Presidential position, or death of the elected President, or loss of Presidential qualification by juridical ruling or other causes, the next President shall be elected within sixty days thereafter.

Article 69

The President shall take the oath of office at the inauguration as follows: "I do solemnly swear to the people that I will faithfully execute the Presidency, with doing my best for observing the Constitution, defending the State, for the peaceful unification of the homeland, for promoting the freedom and welfare of the people, and for developing national culture."

Article 70

The term of the Presidency shall be five years, and the President shall not hold office for consecutive terms.

Article 71

In case of becoming vacant of the Presidential position or not being capable because of an accident, the Prime Minister shall act for the President, and be followed by other members of the State Council in the order as prescribed by acts.

Article 72

The President may put major policies to a referendum related to foreign, defense, unification, and other national security affairs, in case conceding it is necessary.

Article 73

The President shall conclude and ratify treaties; trust and receive letters of credence of foreign delegations; dispatch of domestic delegations to a foreign state; declare war, and; conclude a peace policy.

Article 74

(1) The President shall have the right to command the armed forces as prescribed by the Constitution and acts.
(2) The organization and classification of the armed forces shall be prescribed by acts.

Article 75

The President may issue presidential decrees on any requirements for executing commissioned contents and acts, with defining specific jurisdiction in acts.

Article 76

(1) The President may take a minimum necessary execution financially or economically, or issue orders of having an effect of acts, only in case of requiring urgent measures, and of having no holding time for any session of the National Assembly, regarding the national security or keeping public safe order, at the time of internal worries, external sufferings, the Act of God, or being under any critical crisis of finance or economics.

(2) The President may issue orders, having an effect of acts, in the limited case of requiring urgent measures, and under not being able to have any session of the National Assembly, to preserve the State at the time of critical engagement in war-related to the national security.

(3) The President shall require any approval from the National Assembly after immediately notifying the issued measures and orders thereof in Sections (1) and (2) thereof.

(4) In case of not being able to require approval from the National Assembly thereof, any measures or orders enforceable by acts, executed by the President, shall not be enforceable just at that time; in such case, any act amended or abolished by the order by the President shall be enforceable naturally from the time of disapproval from the National Assembly.

(5) The President shall promulgate the reason for disapproval related to Section (3) and (4) thereof without delay.

Article 77

(1) The President may declare martial laws, as prescribed by acts, in case of being under the requirement of military forces at the time of the war or incident or a state of emergency, or if necessary for keeping public safety and order.

(2) The martial laws shall be classified as martial laws of emergency and martial laws of vigilance.

(3) The President may have the right to execute special measures, at the time of declaring a martial law of emergency, as prescribed by acts, regarding the warrant issuing, the freedom of speech, press, assembly, and association, or any right of the Government and the Court of Korea.

(4) The President shall notify the National Assembly of the declaration of the martial laws without delay at the time of declaring thereof.

(5) The President shall lift the marital laws thereof when the National Assembly requires lifting the martial state by the concurrence of a majority of the enrolled members.

Article 78

The President shall appoint and dismiss public officials as prescribed by the Constitution and acts.

Article 79

(1) The President may grant pardons, remissions of punishment, or rights restoration as prescribed by acts.

(2) The President shall require consent from the National Assembly for granting general pardons.

(3) Requirements for pardons, remissions of punishment, or rights restoration shall be as prescribed by acts.

Article 80

The President shall award decorations and honors as prescribed by acts.

Article 81

The President may attend and address the National Assembly or express written opinions.

Article 82

The President shall execute national affairs, under acts, by written documents, and the Prime Minister and other members of the State Council shall countersign these documents. Any documents related to the execution of military affairs shall be as well.

Article 83

The President shall not hold the office of the Prime Minister, a member of the State Council, a Minister of the Government, or any head of public corporation as prescribed by acts.

Article 84

The President shall not be under any criminal prosecution, except for committing the crime of insurrection or external disaster during the presidency tenure.

Article 85

Status and courtesy for former Presidents shall be prescribed by acts.

SECTION 2. The Administration

SECTION 2-1. The Prime Minister and Members of the State Council

Article 86

(1) The President shall appoint the Prime Minister with the consent of the National Assembly.
(2) The Prime Minister shall assist the President, and preside over every ministry of the Administration under the order of the President for administration.
(3) Any military officer shall not be appointed as the Prime Minister unless being discharged from the military service.

Article 87

(1) The President shall appoint the members of the State Council with the consent of the National Assembly.
(2) The members of the State Council shall assist the President for the State affairs, and deliberate the State affairs as members for the State council meetings.
(3) The Prime Minister may recommend the President to dismiss any member of the State Council.
(4) Any military officer shall not be appointed as a member of the State

Council unless being discharged from the military service.

SECTION 2-2. The State Council

Article 88

(1) The State Council shall deliberate on major policies belonging to the authority of the Government.
(2) The State Council shall be composed of the President, the Prime Minister, and council members of no less than fifteen, and no more than thirty.
(3) The President shall be the Chairperson of the State Council; the Prime Minister shall be the Vice-Chairperson.

Article 89

The State of Council shall deliberate following articles:
1. Fundamental plans for the State affairs and general policies of the Government
2. Declaration of war, peace treaty, and other major foreign policies
3. Proposals for amendments to the Constitution, a national referendum, treaties, legislative bills, and presidential decrees
4. Proposals for the establishment of budgets and accounts, fundamental plans for national property disposition, contracts of being a potential financial burden on the State, and other major articles for national finance
5. Emergency orders; emergent financial and economical disposition and orders; declaration and termination of the martial laws by the President
6. Major articles regarding military affairs
7. Requests for any openings of an extraordinary session of the National Assembly
8. Awarding of honors and promotions
9. Grating pardons, remissions of punishment, and rights restoration
10. Planning and determination of between every authority for ministries of the Government
11. Fundamental plans regarding the delegation and displacement of

authority about any proposals of the Government.
12. Evaluation and analysis of situations of execution for the State affairs
13. Establishment and coordination of major policies belong to every ministry in the Government
14. Filings of the dissolution of political parties
15. Deliberation on petitions regarding policies submitted or referred to the Government
16. Appointment of the Prosecutor General, the Chairperson of the Joint Chiefs of Staff, the Chief of Staff of every armed force, presidents of national universities, ambassadors, other public officers prescribed by acts, and managers of Government enterprises
17. Articles presented by the President, the Prime Minister, and members of the State Council

Article 90

(1) The State Advisory Council of Senior States person, composed of senior state personnel, may be established to counsel the President regarding major articles of state affairs.
(2) The last former President shall be a chairperson of the State Advisory Council of Senior States person; however, in the case of being vacant of last former President, the President shall appoint a chairperson.
(3) The organization, jurisdiction of the authority, and other requirements for the State Advisory Council of Senior States person shall be prescribed by acts.

Article 91

(1) The National Security Council shall be established for advising inquiries from the President, before the deliberation of the State Council, about the foreign, military, and domestic policies related to national security.
(2) The President shall preside over meetings of the National Security Council.
(3) The organization, jurisdiction of the authority, and other requirements for the National Security Council shall be prescribed by acts.

Article 92

(1) The National Unification Advisory Council, for advising inquiries from the President, may be organized regarding the establishment of peaceful unification policies.
(2) The organization, jurisdiction of the authority, and other requirements for the National Unification Advisory Council shall be prescribed by acts.

Article 93

(1) The National Economic Advisory Council, for advising inquiries from the President, may be organized regarding the establishment of major policies for the development of the national economy.
(2) The organization, jurisdiction of the authority, and other requirements for the National Economic Advisory Council shall be prescribed by acts.

SECTION 2-3. Ministries of the Government

Article 94

The President shall appoint each minister of the Government, according to the request from the Prime Minister, among members of the State Council.

Article 95

The Prime Minister and every Minister of the Government may, for official affairs being under the respective jurisdiction, issue ordinances of the Prime Minister or the Minister thereof, by acts or any commissions from the President, or respective official authority.

Article 96

The establishment, organization, and jurisdiction of duty for the respective ministry of the Government shall be prescribed by acts.

SECTION 2-4. The Board of Audit and Inspection

Article 97

The Board of Audit and Inspection shall be established, under the jurisdiction of the President, for the inspection related to a national balance sheet account of revenue and expenditure of the State; to an account audit of the State and authorized organizations prescribed by the acts, and; to the execution of obligation by authorities and public officials of the State.

Article 98

(1) The Board of Audit and Inspection shall consist of no less than five and no more than eleven audit members, including the Chairperson.
(2) The President shall appoint the Chairperson with the consent of the National Assembly. The term of office of the Chairperson shall be four years and may hold office once a consecutive term for four years.
(3) The President shall appoint audit members according to a request from the Chairperson. The term of audit members shall be four years and may hold office once a consecutive term for four years.

Article 99

The Board of Audit and Inspection shall audit a national balance sheet account of revenue and expenditure of the State every fiscal year; and shall report the result to the President and the next session of the National Assembly.

Article 100

The organization, the scope of jurisdiction, the qualification of the members of the Board of Audit and Inspection, the scope of public officials for executing an audit, and other requirements shall be prescribed by acts.

CHAPTER 5. THE COURTS

Article 101

(1) Judicial authority shall be vested in courts consisting of judges.//
(2) The courts shall consist of the Supreme Court, the highest court, and several classified inferior courts.
(3) Qualifications for holding judge status shall be prescribed by acts.

Article 102

(1) Juridical departments may be organized in the Supreme Court.
(2) Supreme Court Judges shall serve in the Supreme Court; however, any judges, who are not in the status of a Supreme Court Judge, may serve in the Supreme Court as prescribed by the acts.
(3) The organization of the Supreme Court and classified inferior courts shall be prescribed by acts.

Article 103

Judges shall judge by the Constitution and act, independently, according to their respective conscience.

Article 104

(1) The President shall appoint the Chief Justice of the Supreme Court with consent from the National Assembly.
(2) The President shall appoint Supreme Court Justices, according to the request of the Chief Justice of the Supreme Court, with the consent of the National Assembly.
(3) For any judges, except the Chief Justice of the Supreme Court and Supreme Court Justices, the Chief Justice of the Supreme Court shall appoint them with the consent of the Conference of Supreme Court Justices.

Article 105

(1) The term of office of the Chief Justice of the Supreme Court shall be six

years, and shall not hold office for consecutive terms.

(2) The term of office of Justices of the Chief Justice shall be six years and may hold office for consecutive terms as prescribed by acts.

(3) The term of office of judges, except the Chief Justice and Justices of the Supreme Court, shall be ten years, and may hold office for consecutive terms as prescribed by acts.

(4) The retirement age of judges shall be prescribed by acts.

Article 106

(1) No Judge shall be dismissed from office unless being under impeachment or sentenced to more than confinement; neither be suspended from office, nor be of salary reduction, or of being under unfavorable treatment unless being punished of discipline.

(2) In case judges are not able to hold office due to critical physical or mental disorders, they may retire from office as prescribed by acts.

Article 107

(1) In case any acts need to be confirmed constitutional, as being a precondition for ruling, the court shall request the Constitutional Court to rule related act thereof is constitutional; and shall judge according to the ruling by the Constitution Court.

(2) In case any decrees, regulations, or dispositions need to be confirmed as legal or constitutional, as being a precondition for ruling, the Supreme Court has the final authority for judicial scrutiny.

(3) Administrative appeals may be proceeding, as of a pre-juridical procedure, before a judicial ruling. The procedure of administrative appeals shall be prescribed by acts; and shall adopt a judicial ruling process.

Article 108

The Supreme Court may establish, within the scope of not violating acts, the procedures of lawsuits, internal discipline rules in court, and rules for administration processing.

Article 109

Hearings and rulings of lawsuits shall be publicity; however, in case of being concerned about national security, disturbing public peaceful order, or impairing good custom, any hearing thereon may not be publicity by the judgment of related courts.

Article 110

(1) Military Courts may be established, as of being special courts, for jurisdiction over the court-martial.
(2) The Supreme Court shall have jurisdiction over the final appeal for military courts.
(3) The organization, authorization, and qualification of judges for Military Courts shall be prescribed by acts.
(4) For military courts under extraordinary martial law, in case of committing crimes by military people and military employees; of committing military spying; of crimes, prescribed by acts, regarding guard-duty military people, guarding posts, poisoned food, or prisoners of war, the ruling may be executed at the first trial. However, for the ruling of capital sentences at the first verdict, that ruling may not be closed at the first trial.

CHAPTER 6. THE CONSTITUTIONAL COURT

Article 111

(1) The Constitutionals Court shall have jurisdiction over trials as follows:
   1. Constitutional adjudication over any acts requested from the courts
   2. Adjudication over impeachment
   3. Adjudication over the dissolution of any political party
   4. Adjudication over any authorization disputes between mutual States, between State agencies and local governments, and between mutual local governments
   5. Adjudication over any constitutional petition prescribed by acts

(2) The Constitutional Court shall consist of nine justices and qualifying judges; the President shall appoint judges for the Constitutional Court.

(3) Among judges appointed according to Section (2) thereof, the National Assembly shall select three judges; the Chief Justice of the Supreme Court shall designate three judges.

(4) The President shall appoint the Chief Justice of the Constitutional Court with consent from the National Assembly.

Article 112

(1) The term of office for Justices of the Constitutional Court shall be six years and may hold office for consecutive terms as prescribed by acts.

(2) The Justices of the Constitutional Court shall not join any political party, nor be involved in any political activities.

(3) No Justice of the Constitutional Court shall be dismissed from office except being impeached or sentenced to criminal punishment of confinement or higher than that.

Article 113

(1) For the decision to the constitutionality of any act; of impeachment; of political party dissolution, and; of citation decision for constitution petition, no less than six Justices of the Constitutional Court shall approve the decision thereto.

(2) The Constitutional Court may establish, within the scope of not violating acts, the procedure of adjudication, internal discipline regulations in court, and regulations for administration processing.

(3) The organization, management, and other requirements for the Constitutional Court shall be prescribed by acts.

CHAPTER 7. NATIONAL ELECTION COMMISSION

Article 114

(1) The National Election Commission shall be established for the fair

management of elections, national referendums, and administration related to political parties.

(2) The National Election Commission shall consist of three members appointed by the President, three members selected by the National Assembly, and three members designated by the Chief Justice of the Supreme Court. A mutuality voting shall elect the Chairperson of the National Election Commission.

(3) The term of office of members of the National Election Commission shall be six years.

(4) The members of the National Election Commission shall not join any political parties, nor be involved in any political activities.

(5) No member of the Commission shall be dismissed from office except being Impeached or sentenced to criminal punishment of confinement or higher than that.

(6) The National Election Commission may establish, within the scope of acts and decrees, regulations regarding the management of elections, national referendums, and administration of political parties; may establish regulations, within the scope of not violating acts, for internal discipline.

(7) The organization, scope of official obligations, and other requirements for classified election commissions shall be prescribed by acts.

Article 115

(1) Every classified election commission may issue necessary instructions to related administration agencies regarding electoral registers, administration for elections and national referendums, and other requirements.

(2) Any administration agencies shall comply with the instructions in Section (1) thereof.

Article 116

(1) Election campaigns shall be within the scope, prescribed by acts, under the management of every classified election commission; shall be guaranteed with equal opportunity.

(2) Election expenses shall not be imposed upon parties or electoral candidates except otherwise prescribed by acts.

CHAPTER 8. LOCAL AUTONOMY GOVERNMENT

Article 117

(1) Local governments may administrate affairs of welfare on residents; manage local government assets, and establish regulations within the acts and decrees.

(2) The classification of local government shall be prescribed by acts.

Article 118

(1) Local Assemblies shall be established in local governments.

(2) The organization and authority of local assemblies, regulations for the election of local assembly members, and heads of local government and organization, and administration of local government shall be prescribed by acts.

CHAPTER 9. THE ECONOMY

Article 119

(1) The economic order of the Republic of Korea shall be based on respect for economic freedom and the creativity of individuals and firms.

(2) The State may maintain balanced national economic growth, stability, and moderate distribution of income; may prevent market domination and economic power abuse; may regulate and coordinate the economy, by the harmony between economic units, for the democratic economy.

Article 120

(1) The State may grant patent protection for extraction, development, and utilization, for a certain period, prescribed by acts, regarding minerals,

any important underground resources, marine resources, hydraulic power, and economically valuable natural power.

(2) The State shall protect the land and resources; and shall establish all necessary plans for the balanced development and utilization thereof.

Article 121

(1) The State shall make an effort to succeed in the realization of principles of Land-to-the-Tiller regarding farmland; any farm tenant institutions shall not be permitted.
(2) The lease and trust management of farmland, for the promotion of agricultural productivity, reasonable utilization, or for being under inevitable conditions, may be approved as prescribed by acts.

Article 122

The State may impose any necessary restrictions and obligations, for effective and balanced utilization, development, and preservation of land, which will be the fundamental necessity for productivity and livelihood of all people, as prescribed by acts.

Article 123

(1) The State shall establish and execute necessary plans of the general development and support, to protect and promote farming and marine products.
(2) The State shall be obliged to promote the local economy for the balanced development between local areas.
(3) The State shall protect and promote medium and small-sized enterprises.
(4) The State shall protect the profit of the people participating in the farming and marine industry, by planning price stability, for the balancing between supply and demand, and the improvement of distribution structure.
(5) The State shall promote independent cooperation organizations of the people participating in the farming and marine industry, and of medium and small-sized enterprises; shall secure their voluntary activities and development.

Article 124

The State shall secure the consumer protection movement for guiding safe consumption, and for the stimulation of product quality improvement, as prescribed by acts,

Article 125

The State may promote trade with foreign states; and may restrict and coordinate thereof.

Article 126

The State shall not nationalize private enterprises or transform them as public assets, nor control or manage thereof, unless for the national defense or urgent necessity in the national economy, as prescribed by acts.

Article 127

(1) The State shall make an effort to develop the national economy by the innovation of science and technology, along with the progress of information and human resources.
(2) The State shall establish the National Standard System.
(3) The President may establish necessary advisory organizations to accomplish the purpose thereof in Section (1).

CHAPTER 10. CONSTITUTIONAL AMENDMENTS

Article 128

(1) Amendments to the Constitution shall be proposed by either a majority of enrolled members of the National Assembly or the President.
(2) Amendments to the Constitution for term extension or consecutive terms of the President shall not be effective for the incumbent President at the time of the proposals of the Constitutional Amendments thereon.

Article 129

Amendments to the Constitution proposed thereof shall be publicly announced for no less than twenty days.

Article 130

(1) The National Assembly shall approve the proposed bills of amendments to the Constitution within sixty days from the date of public announcement; the concurrence from the National Assembly shall require a two-thirds majority vote to pass the bills.

(2) The bills, as of amendments to the Constitution, concurred from the National Assembly shall be submitted to a national referendum within thirty days after the day of the concurrence; shall require, for being ratified, a majority vote from a majority electorate eligible for the National Assembly election.

(3) The bills of Constitutional amendments shall be ratified by the concurrence from the vote in Section (2) thereof, and the President shall promulgate the ratified amendments without delay.

대한민국헌법

[시행 1988. 2. 25.] [헌법 제10호, 1987. 10. 29., 전부개정]

전문

유구한 역사와 전통에 빛나는 우리 대한국민은 3·1운동으로 건립된 대한민국임시정부의 법통과 불의에 항거한 4·19민주이념을 계승하고, 조국의 민주개혁과 평화적 통일의 사명에 입각하여 정의·인도와 동포애로써 민족의 단결을 공고히 하고, 모든 사회적 폐습과 불의를 타파하며, 자율과 조화를 바탕으로 자유민주적 기본질서를 더욱 확고히 하여 정치·경제·사회·문화의 모든 영역에 있어서 각인의 기회를 균등히 하고, 능력을 최고도로 발휘하게 하며, 자유와 권리에 따르는 책임과 의무를 완수하게 하여, 안으로는 국민생활의 균등한 향상을 기하고 밖으로는 항구적인 세계평화와 인류공영에 이바지함으로써 우리들과 우리들의 자손의 안전과 자유와 행복을 영원히 확보할 것을 다짐하면서 1948년 7월 12일에 제정되고 8차에 걸쳐 개정된 헌법을 이제 국회의 의결을 거쳐 국민투표에 의하여 개정한다.

제 1 장 총 강

제 1 조 ①대한민국은 민주공화국이다.
②대한민국의 주권은 국민에게 있고, 모든 권력은 국민으로부터 나온다.
제 2 조 ①대한민국의 국민이 되는 요건은 법률로 정한다.
②국가는 법률이 정하는 바에 의하여 재외국민을 보호할 의무를 진다.
제 3 조 대한민국의 영토는 한반도와 그 부속도서로 한다.
제 4 조 대한민국은 통일을 지향하며, 자유민주적 기본질서에 입각한 평화적 통일 정책을 수립하고 이를 추진한다.
제 5 조 ①대한민국은 국제평화의 유지에 노력하고 침략적 전쟁을 부인한다.
②국군은 국가의 안전보장과 국토방위의 신성한 의무를 수행함을 사명으로 하며, 그 정치적 중립성은 준수된다.

제 6 조 ①헌법에 의하여 체결·공포된 조약과 일반적으로 승인된 국제법규는 국내법과 같은 효력을 가진다.

②외국인은 국제법과 조약이 정하는 바에 의하여 그 지위가 보장된다.

제 7 조 ①공무원은 국민전체에 대한 봉사자이며, 국민에 대하여 책임을 진다.

②공무원의 신분과 정치적 중립성은 법률이 정하는 바에 의하여 보장된다.

제 8 조 ①정당의 설립은 자유이며, 복수정당제는 보장된다.

②정당은 그 목적·조직과 활동이 민주적이어야 하며, 국민의 정치적 의사형성에 참여하는데 필요한 조직을 가져야 한다.

③정당은 법률이 정하는 바에 의하여 국가의 보호를 받으며, 국가는 법률이 정하는 바에 의하여 정당운영에 필요한 자금을 보조할 수 있다.

④정당의 목적이나 활동이 민주적 기본질서에 위배될 때에는 정부는 헌법재판소에 그 해산을 제소할 수 있고, 정당은 헌법재판소의 심판에 의하여 해산된다.

제 9 조 국가는 전통문화의 계승·발전과 민족문화의 창달에 노력하여야 한다.

제 2 장 국민의 권리와 의무

제10조 모든 국민은 인간으로서의 존엄과 가치를 가지며, 행복을 추구할 권리를 가진다. 국가는 개인이 가지는 불가침의 기본적 인권을 확인하고 이를 보장할 의무를 진다.

제11조 ①모든 국민은 법 앞에 평등하다. 누구든지 성별·종교 또는 사회적 신분에 의하여 정치적·경제적·사회적·문화적 생활의 모든 영역에 있어서 차별을 받지 아니한다.

②사회적 특수계급의 제도는 인정되지 아니하며, 어떠한 형태로도 이를 창설할 수 없다.

③훈장 등의 영전은 이를 받은 자에게만 효력이 있고, 어떠한 특권도 이에 따르지 아니한다.

제12조 ①모든 국민은 신체의 자유를 가진다. 누구든지 법률에 의하지 아니하고는 체포·구속·압수·수색 또는 심문을 받지 아니하며, 법률과 적법한 절차에 의하지 아니하고는 처벌·보안처분 또는 강제노역을 받지 아니한다.

②모든 국민은 고문을 받지 아니하며, 형사상 자기에게 불리한 진술을 강요당하

지 아니한다.

③체포·구속·압수 또는 수색을 할 때에는 적법한 절차에 따라 검사의 신청에 의하여 법관이 발부한 영장을 제시하여야 한다. 다만, 현행범인인 경우와 장기 3년 이상의 형에 해당하는 죄를 범하고 도피 또는 증거인멸의 염려가 있을 때에는 사후에 영장을 청구할 수 있다.

④누구든지 체포 또는 구속을 당한 때에는 즉시 변호인의 조력을 받을 권리를 가진다. 다만, 형사피고인이 스스로 변호인을 구할 수 없을 때에는 법률이 정하는 바에 의하여 국가가 변호인을 붙인다.

⑤누구든지 체포 또는 구속의 이유와 변호인의 조력을 받을 권리가 있음을 고지받지 아니하고는 체포 또는 구속을 당하지 아니한다. 체포 또는 구속을 당한 자의 가족등 법률이 정하는 자에게는 그 이유와 일시·장소가 지체없이 통지되어야 한다.

⑥누구든지 체포 또는 구속을 당한 때에는 적부의 심사를 법원에 청구할 권리를 가진다.

⑦피고인의 자백이 고문·폭행·협박·구속의 부당한 장기화 또는 기망 기타의 방법에 의하여 자의로 진술된 것이 아니라고 인정될 때 또는 정식재판에 있어서 피고인의 자백이 그에게 불리한 유일한 증거일 때에는 이를 유죄의 증거로 삼거나 이를 이유로 처벌할 수 없다.

제13조 ①모든 국민은 행위시의 법률에 의하여 범죄를 구성하지 아니하는 행위로 소추되지 아니하며, 동일한 범죄에 대하여 거듭 처벌받지 아니한다.

②모든 국민은 소급입법에 의하여 참정권의 제한을 받거나 재산권을 박탈당하지 아니한다.

③모든 국민은 자기의 행위가 아닌 친족의 행위로 인하여 불이익한 처우를 받지 아니한다.

제14조 모든 국민은 거주·이전의 자유를 가진다.

제15조 모든 국민은 직업선택의 자유를 가진다.

제16조 모든 국민은 주거의 자유를 침해받지 아니한다. 주거에 대한 압수나 수색을 할 때에는 검사의 신청에 의하여 법관이 발부한 영장을 제시하여야 한다.

제17조 모든 국민은 사생활의 비밀과 자유를 침해받지 아니한다.

제18조 모든 국민은 통신의 비밀을 침해받지 아니한다.

제19조 모든 국민은 양심의 자유를 가진다.

제20조 ①모든 국민은 종교의 자유를 가진다.

②국교는 인정되지 아니하며, 종교와 정치는 분리된다.

제21조 ①모든 국민은 언론·출판의 자유와 집회·결사의 자유를 가진다.

②언론·출판에 대한 허가나 검열과 집회·결사에 대한 허가는 인정되지 아니한다.

③통신·방송의 시설기준과 신문의 기능을 보장하기 위하여 필요한 사항은 법률로 정한다.

④언론·출판은 타인의 명예나 권리 또는 공중도덕이나 사회윤리를 침해하여서는 아니된다. 언론·출판이 타인의 명예나 권리를 침해한 때에는 피해자는 이에 대한 피해의 배상을 청구할 수 있다.

제22조 ①모든 국민은 학문과 예술의 자유를 가진다.

②저작자·발명가·과학기술자와 예술가의 권리는 법률로써 보호한다.

제23조 ①모든 국민의 재산권은 보장된다. 그 내용과 한계는 법률로 정한다.

②재산권의 행사는 공공복리에 적합하도록 하여야 한다.

③공공필요에 의한 재산권의 수용·사용 또는 제한 및 그에 대한 보상은 법률로써 하되, 정당한 보상을 지급하여야 한다.

제24조 모든 국민은 법률이 정하는 바에 의하여 선거권을 가진다.

제25조 모든 국민은 법률이 정하는 바에 의하여 공무담임권을 가진다.

제26조 ①모든 국민은 법률이 정하는 바에 의하여 국가기관에 문서로 청원할 권리를 가진다.

②국가는 청원에 대하여 심사할 의무를 진다.

제27조 ①모든 국민은 헌법과 법률이 정한 법관에 의하여 법률에 의한 재판을 받을 권리를 가진다.

②군인 또는 군무원이 아닌 국민은 대한민국의 영역 안에서는 중대한 군사상 기밀·초병·초소·유독음식물공급·포로·군용물에 관한 죄중 법률이 정한 경우와 비상계엄이 선포된 경우를 제외하고는 군사법원의 재판을 받지 아니한다.

③모든 국민은 신속한 재판을 받을 권리를 가진다. 형사피고인은 상당한 이유가 없는 한 지체없이 공개재판을 받을 권리를 가진다.

④형사피고인은 유죄의 판결이 확정될 때까지는 무죄로 추정된다.

⑤형사피해자는 법률이 정하는 바에 의하여 당해 사건의 재판절차에서 진술할 수 있다.

제28조 형사피의자 또는 형사피고인으로서 구금되었던 자가 법률이 정하는 불기

소처분을 받거나 무죄판결을 받은 때에는 법률이 정하는 바에 의하여 국가에 정당한 보상을 청구할 수 있다.

제29조 ①공무원의 직무상 불법행위로 손해를 받은 국민은 법률이 정하는 바에 의하여 국가 또는 공공단체에 정당한 배상을 청구할 수 있다. 이 경우 공무원 자신의 책임은 면제되지 아니한다.
②군인·군무원·경찰공무원 기타 법률이 정하는 자가 전투·훈련등 직무집행과 관련하여 받은 손해에 대하여는 법률이 정하는 보상 외에 국가 또는 공공단체에 공무원의 직무상 불법행위로 인한 배상은 청구할 수 없다.

제30조 타인의 범죄행위로 인하여 생명·신체에 대한 피해를 받은 국민은 법률이 정하는 바에 의하여 국가로부터 구조를 받을 수 있다.

제31조 ①모든 국민은 능력에 따라 균등하게 교육을 받을 권리를 가진다.
②모든 국민은 그 보호하는 자녀에게 적어도 초등교육과 법률이 정하는 교육을 받게 할 의무를 진다.
③의무교육은 무상으로 한다.
④교육의 자주성·전문성·정치적 중립성 및 대학의 자율성은 법률이 정하는 바에 의하여 보장된다.
⑤국가는 평생교육을 진흥하여야 한다.
⑥학교교육 및 평생교육을 포함한 교육제도와 그 운영, 교육재정 및 교원의 지위에 관한 기본적인 사항은 법률로 정한다.

제32조 ①모든 국민은 근로의 권리를 가진다. 국가는 사회적·경제적 방법으로 근로자의 고용의 증진과 적정임금의 보장에 노력하여야 하며, 법률이 정하는 바에 의하여 최저임금제를 시행하여야 한다.
②모든 국민은 근로의 의무를 진다. 국가는 근로의 의무의 내용과 조건을 민주주의원칙에 따라 법률로 정한다.
③근로조건의 기준은 인간의 존엄성을 보장하도록 법률로 정한다.
④여자의 근로는 특별한 보호를 받으며, 고용·임금 및 근로조건에 있어서 부당한 차별을 받지 아니한다.
⑤연소자의 근로는 특별한 보호를 받는다.
⑥국가유공자·상이군경 및 전몰군경의 유가족은 법률이 정하는 바에 의하여 우선적으로 근로의 기회를 부여받는다.

제33조 ①근로자는 근로조건의 향상을 위하여 자주적인 단결권·단체교섭권 및

단체행동권을 가진다.

②공무원인 근로자는 법률이 정하는 자에 한하여 단결권·단체교섭권 및 단체행동권을 가진다.

③법률이 정하는 주요방위산업체에 종사하는 근로자의 단체행동권은 법률이 정하는 바에 의하여 이를 제한하거나 인정하지 아니할 수 있다.

제34조 ①모든 국민은 인간다운 생활을 할 권리를 가진다.

②국가는 사회보장·사회복지의 증진에 노력할 의무를 진다.

③국가는 여자의 복지와 권익의 향상을 위하여 노력하여야 한다.

④국가는 노인과 청소년의 복지향상을 위한 정책을 실시할 의무를 진다.

⑤신체장애자 및 질병·노령 기타의 사유로 생활능력이 없는 국민은 법률이 정하는 바에 의하여 국가의 보호를 받는다.

⑥국가는 재해를 예방하고 그 위험으로부터 국민을 보호하기 위하여 노력하여야 한다.

제35조 ①모든 국민은 건강하고 쾌적한 환경에서 생활할 권리를 가지며, 국가와 국민은 환경보전을 위하여 노력하여야 한다.

②환경권의 내용과 행사에 관하여는 법률로 정한다.

③국가는 주택개발정책등을 통하여 모든 국민이 쾌적한 주거생활을 할 수 있도록 노력하여야 한다.

제36조 ①혼인과 가족생활은 개인의 존엄과 양성의 평등을 기초로 성립되고 유지되어야 하며, 국가는 이를 보장한다.

②국가는 모성의 보호를 위하여 노력하여야 한다.

③모든 국민은 보건에 관하여 국가의 보호를 받는다.

제37조 ①국민의 자유와 권리는 헌법에 열거되지 아니한 이유로 경시되지 아니한다.

②국민의 모든 자유와 권리는 국가안전보장·질서유지 또는 공공복리를 위하여 필요한 경우에 한하여 법률로써 제한할 수 있으며, 제한하는 경우에도 자유와 권리의 본질적인 내용을 침해할 수 없다.

제38조 모든 국민은 법률이 정하는 바에 의하여 납세의 의무를 진다.

제39조 ①모든 국민은 법률이 정하는 바에 의하여 국방의 의무를 진다.

②누구든지 병역의무의 이행으로 인하여 불이익한 처우를 받지 아니한다.

제3장 국회

제40조 입법권은 국회에 속한다.

제41조 ①국회는 국민의 보통·평등·직접·비밀선거에 의하여 선출된 국회의원으로 구성한다.

②국회의원의 수는 법률로 정하되, 200인 이상으로 한다.

③국회의원의 선거구와 비례대표제 기타 선거에 관한 사항은 법률로 정한다.

제42조 국회의원의 임기는 4년으로 한다.

제43조 국회의원은 법률이 정하는 직을 겸할 수 없다.

제44조 ①국회의원은 현행범인인 경우를 제외하고는 회기 중 국회의 동의없이 체포 또는 구금되지 아니한다.

②국회의원이 회기 전에 체포 또는 구금된 때에는 현행범인이 아닌 한 국회의 요구가 있으면 회기 중 석방된다.

제45조 국회의원은 국회에서 직무상 행한 발언과 표결에 관하여 국회 외에서 책임을 지지 아니한다.

제46조 ①국회의원은 청렴의 의무가 있다.

②국회의원은 국가이익을 우선하여 양심에 따라 직무를 행한다.

③국회의원은 그 지위를 남용하여 국가·공공단체 또는 기업체와의 계약이나 그 처분에 의하여 재산상의 권리·이익 또는 직위를 취득하거나 타인을 위하여 그 취득을 알선할 수 없다.

제47조 ①국회의 정기회는 법률이 정하는 바에 의하여 매년 1회 집회되며, 국회의 임시회는 대통령 또는 국회재적의원 4분의 1 이상의 요구에 의하여 집회된다.

②정기회의 회기는 100일을, 임시회의 회기는 30일을 초과할 수 없다.

③대통령이 임시회의 집회를 요구할 때에는 기간과 집회요구의 이유를 명시하여야 한다.

제48조 국회는 의장 1인과 부의장 2인을 선출한다.

제49조 국회는 헌법 또는 법률에 특별한 규정이 없는 한 재적의원 과반수의 출석과 출석의원 과반수의 찬성으로 의결한다. 가부동수인 때에는 부결된 것으로 본다.

제50조 ①국회의 회의는 공개한다. 다만, 출석의원 과반수의 찬성이 있거나 의장이 국가의 안전보장을 위하여 필요하다고 인정할 때에는 공개하지 아니할 수 있다.

②공개하지 아니한 회의내용의 공표에 관하여는 법률이 정하는 바에 의한다.

제51조 국회에 제출된 법률안 기타의 의안은 회기 중에 의결되지 못한 이유로 폐기되지 아니한다. 다만, 국회의원의 임기가 만료된 때에는 그러하지 아니하다.

제52조 국회의원과 정부는 법률안을 제출할 수 있다.

제53조 ①국회에서 의결된 법률안은 정부에 이송되어 15일 이내에 대통령이 공포한다.

②법률안에 이의가 있을 때에는 대통령은 제1항의 기간내에 이의서를 붙여 국회로 환부하고, 그 재의를 요구할 수 있다. 국회의 폐회 중에도 또한 같다.

③대통령은 법률안의 일부에 대하여 또는 법률안을 수정하여 재의를 요구할 수 없다.

④재의의 요구가 있을 때에는 국회는 재의에 붙이고, 재적의원 과반수의 출석과 출석의원 3분의 2 이상의 찬성으로 전과 같은 의결을 하면 그 법률안은 법률로서 확정된다.

⑤대통령이 제1항의 기간 내에 공포나 재의의 요구를 하지 아니한 때에도 그 법률안은 법률로서 확정된다.

⑥대통령은 제4항과 제5항의 규정에 의하여 확정된 법률을 지체없이 공포하여야 한다. 제5항에 의하여 법률이 확정된 후 또는 제4항에 의한 확정법률이 정부에 이송된 후 5일 이내에 대통령이 공포하지 아니할 때에는 국회의장이 이를 공포한다.

⑦법률은 특별한 규정이 없는 한 공포한 날로부터 20일을 경과함으로써 효력을 발생한다.

제54조 ①국회는 국가의 예산안을 심의·확정한다.

②정부는 회계연도마다 예산안을 편성하여 회계연도 개시 90일 전까지 국회에 제출하고, 국회는 회계연도 개시 30일 전까지 이를 의결하여야 한다.

③새로운 회계연도가 개시될 때까지 예산안이 의결되지 못한 때에는 정부는 국회에서 예산안이 의결될 때까지 다음의 목적을 위한 경비는 전년도 예산에 준하여 집행할 수 있다.

1. 헌법이나 법률에 의하여 설치된 기관 또는 시설의 유지·운영
2. 법률상 지출의무의 이행
3. 이미 예산으로 승인된 사업의 계속

제55조 ①한 회계연도를 넘어 계속하여 지출할 필요가 있을 때에는 정부는 연한을 정하여 계속비로서 국회의 의결을 얻어야 한다.

②예비비는 총액으로 국회의 의결을 얻어야 한다. 예비비의 지출은 차기국회의

승인을 얻어야 한다.

제56조 정부는 예산에 변경을 가할 필요가 있을 때에는 추가경정예산안을 편성하여 국회에 제출할 수 있다.

제57조 국회는 정부의 동의 없이 정부가 제출한 지출예산 각항의 금액을 증가하거나 새 비목을 설치할 수 없다.

제58조 국채를 모집하거나 예산 외에 국가의 부담이 될 계약을 체결하려 할 때에는 정부는 미리 국회의 의결을 얻어야 한다.

제59조 조세의 종목과 세율은 법률로 정한다.

제60조 ①국회는 상호원조 또는 안전보장에 관한 조약, 중요한 국제조직에 관한 조약, 우호통상항해조약, 주권의 제약에 관한 조약, 강화조약, 국가나 국민에게 중대한 재정적 부담을 지우는 조약 또는 입법사항에 관한 조약의 체결·비준에 대한 동의권을 가진다.
②국회는 선전포고, 국군의 외국에의 파견 또는 외국군대의 대한민국 영역 안에서의 주류에 대한 동의권을 가진다.

제61조 ①국회는 국정을 감사하거나 특정한 국정사안에 대하여 조사할 수 있으며, 이에 필요한 서류의 제출 또는 증인의 출석과 증언이나 의견의 진술을 요구할 수 있다.
②국정감사 및 조사에 관한 절차 기타 필요한 사항은 법률로 정한다.

제62조 ①국무총리·국무위원 또는 정부위원은 국회나 그 위원회에 출석하여 국정처리상황을 보고하거나 의견을 진술하고 질문에 응답할 수 있다.
②국회나 그 위원회의 요구가 있을 때에는 국무총리·국무위원 또는 정부위원은 출석·답변하여야 하며, 국무총리 또는 국무위원이 출석요구를 받은 때에는 국무위원 또는 정부위원으로 하여금 출석·답변하게 할 수 있다.

제63조 ①국회는 국무총리 또는 국무위원의 해임을 대통령에게 건의할 수 있다.
②제1항의 해임건의는 국회재적의원 3분의 1 이상의 발의에 의하여 국회재적의원 과반수의 찬성이 있어야 한다.

제64조 ①국회는 법률에 저촉되지 아니하는 범위 안에서 의사와 내부규율에 관한 규칙을 제정할 수 있다.
②국회는 의원의 자격을 심사하며, 의원을 징계할 수 있다.
③의원을 제명하려면 국회재적의원 3분의 2 이상의 찬성이 있어야 한다.
④제2항과 제3항의 처분에 대하여는 법원에 제소할 수 없다.

제65조 ①대통령·국무총리·국무위원·행정각부의 장·헌법재판소 재판관·법관·중앙선거관리위원회 위원·감사원장·감사위원 기타 법률이 정한 공무원이 그 직무집행에 있어서 헌법이나 법률을 위배한 때에는 국회는 탄핵의 소추를 의결할 수 있다.

②제1항의 탄핵소추는 국회재적의원 3분의 1 이상의 발의가 있어야 하며, 그 의결은 국회재적의원 과반수의 찬성이 있어야 한다. 다만, 대통령에 대한 탄핵소추는 국회재적의원 과반수의 발의와 국회재적의원 3분의 2 이상의 찬성이 있어야 한다.

③탄핵소추의 의결을 받은 자는 탄핵심판이 있을 때까지 그 권한행사가 정지된다.

④탄핵결정은 공직으로부터 파면함에 그친다. 그러나, 이에 의하여 민사상이나 형사상의 책임이 면제되지는 아니한다.

제 4 장 정부

제1절 대통령

제66조 ①대통령은 국가의 원수이며, 외국에 대하여 국가를 대표한다.

②대통령은 국가의 독립·영토의 보전·국가의 계속성과 헌법을 수호할 책무를 진다.

③대통령은 조국의 평화적 통일을 위한 성실한 의무를 진다.

④행정권은 대통령을 수반으로 하는 정부에 속한다.

제67조 ①대통령은 국민의 보통·평등·직접·비밀선거에 의하여 선출한다.

②제1항의 선거에 있어서 최고득표자가 2인 이상인 때에는 국회의 재적의원 과반수가 출석한 공개회의에서 다수표를 얻은 자를 당선자로 한다.

③대통령후보자가 1인일 때에는 그 득표수가 선거권자 총수의 3분의 1 이상이 아니면 대통령으로 당선될 수 없다.

④대통령으로 선거될 수 있는 자는 국회의원의 피선거권이 있고 선거일 현재 40세에 달하여야 한다.

⑤대통령의 선거에 관한 사항은 법률로 정한다.

제68조 ①대통령의 임기가 만료되는 때에는 임기만료 70일 내지 40일 전에 후임자를 선거한다.

②대통령이 궐위된 때 또는 대통령 당선자가 사망하거나 판결 기타의 사유로 그 자격을 상실한 때에는 60일 이내에 후임자를 선거한다.

제69조 대통령은 취임에 즈음하여 다음의 선서를 한다.

"나는 헌법을 준수하고 국가를 보위하며 조국의 평화적 통일과 국민의 자유와 복리의 증진 및 민족문화의 창달에 노력하여 대통령으로서의 직책을 성실히 수행할 것을 국민 앞에 엄숙히 선서합니다."

제70조 대통령의 임기는 5년으로 하며, 중임할 수 없다.

제71조 대통령이 궐위되거나 사고로 인하여 직무를 수행할 수 없을 때에는 국무총리, 법률이 정한 국무위원의 순서로 그 권한을 대행한다.

제72조 대통령은 필요하다고 인정할 때에는 외교·국방·통일 기타 국가안위에 관한 중요정책을 국민투표에 붙일 수 있다.

제73조 대통령은 조약을 체결·비준하고, 외교사절을 신임·접수 또는 파견하며, 선전포고와 강화를 한다.

제74조 ①대통령은 헌법과 법률이 정하는 바에 의하여 국군을 통수한다.

②국군의 조직과 편성은 법률로 정한다.

제75조 대통령은 법률에서 구체적으로 범위를 정하여 위임받은 사항과 법률을 집행하기 위하여 필요한 사항에 관하여 대통령령을 발할 수 있다.

제76조 ①대통령은 내우·외환·천재·지변 또는 중대한 재정·경제상의 위기에 있어서 국가의 안전보장 또는 공공의 안녕질서를 유지하기 위하여 긴급한 조치가 필요하고 국회의 집회를 기다릴 여유가 없을 때에 한하여 최소한으로 필요한 재정·경제상의 처분을 하거나 이에 관하여 법률의 효력을 가지는 명령을 발할 수 있다.

②대통령은 국가의 안위에 관계되는 중대한 교전상태에 있어서 국가를 보위하기 위하여 긴급한 조치가 필요하고 국회의 집회가 불가능한 때에 한하여 법률의 효력을 가지는 명령을 발할 수 있다.

③대통령은 제1항과 제2항의 처분 또는 명령을 한 때에는 지체없이 국회에 보고하여 그 승인을 얻어야 한다.

④제3항의 승인을 얻지 못한 때에는 그 처분 또는 명령은 그때부터 효력을 상실한다. 이 경우 그 명령에 의하여 개정 또는 폐지되었던 법률은 그 명령이 승인을 얻지 못한 때부터 당연히 효력을 회복한다.

⑤대통령은 제3항과 제4항의 사유를 지체없이 공포하여야 한다.

제77조 ①대통령은 전시·사변 또는 이에 준하는 국가비상사태에 있어서 병력으로써 군사상의 필요에 응하거나 공공의 안녕질서를 유지할 필요가 있을 때에는 법률이 정하는 바에 의하여 계엄을 선포할 수 있다.

②계엄은 비상계엄과 경비계엄으로 한다.

③비상계엄이 선포된 때에는 법률이 정하는 바에 의하여 영장제도, 언론·출판·집회·결사의 자유, 정부나 법원의 권한에 관하여 특별한 조치를 할 수 있다.

④계엄을 선포한 때에는 대통령은 지체없이 국회에 통고하여야 한다.

⑤국회가 재적의원 과반수의 찬성으로 계엄의 해제를 요구한 때에는 대통령은 이를 해제하여야 한다.

제78조 대통령은 헌법과 법률이 정하는 바에 의하여 공무원을 임면한다.

제79조 ①대통령은 법률이 정하는 바에 의하여 사면·감형 또는 복권을 명할 수 있다.

②일반사면을 명하려면 국회의 동의를 얻어야 한다.

③사면·감형 및 복권에 관한 사항은 법률로 정한다.

제80조 대통령은 법률이 정하는 바에 의하여 훈장 기타의 영전을 수여한다.

제81조 대통령은 국회에 출석하여 발언하거나 서한으로 의견을 표시할 수 있다.

제82조 대통령의 국법상 행위는 문서로써 하며, 이 문서에는 국무총리와 관계 국무위원이 부서한다. 군사에 관한 것도 또한 같다.

제83조 대통령은 국무총리·국무위원·행정각부의 장 기타 법률이 정하는 공사의 직을 겸할 수 없다.

제84조 대통령은 내란 또는 외환의 죄를 범한 경우를 제외하고는 재직 중 형사상의 소추를 받지 아니한다.

제85조 전직대통령의 신분과 예우에 관하여는 법률로 정한다.

제2절 행정부

제1관 국무총리와 국무위원

제86조 ①국무총리는 국회의 동의를 얻어 대통령이 임명한다.

②국무총리는 대통령을 보좌하며, 행정에 관하여 대통령의 명을 받아 행정각부를 통할한다.

③군인은 현역을 면한 후가 아니면 국무총리로 임명될 수 없다.

제87조 ①국무위원은 국무총리의 제청으로 대통령이 임명한다.

②국무위원은 국정에 관하여 대통령을 보좌하며, 국무회의의 구성원으로서 국정을 심의한다.

③국무총리는 국무위원의 해임을 대통령에게 건의할 수 있다.

④군인은 현역을 면한 후가 아니면 국무위원으로 임명될 수 없다.

제2관 국무회의

제88조 ①국무회의는 정부의 권한에 속하는 중요한 정책을 심의한다.

②국무회의는 대통령·국무총리와 15인 이상 30인 이하의 국무위원으로 구성한다.

③대통령은 국무회의의 의장이 되고, 국무총리는 부의장이 된다.

제89조 다음 사항은 국무회의의 심의를 거쳐야 한다.

1. 국정의 기본계획과 정부의 일반정책
2. 선전·강화 기타 중요한 대외정책
3. 헌법개정안·국민투표안·조약안·법률안 및 대통령령안
4. 예산안·결산·국유재산처분의 기본계획·국가의 부담이 될 계약 기타 재정에 관한 중요사항
5. 대통령의 긴급명령·긴급재정경제처분 및 명령 또는 계엄과 그 해제
6. 군사에 관한 중요사항
7. 국회의 임시회 집회의 요구
8. 영전수여
9. 사면·감형과 복권
10. 행정각부간의 권한의 획정
11. 정부 안의 권한의 위임 또는 배정에 관한 기본계획
12. 국정처리상황의 평가·분석
13. 행정각부의 중요한 정책의 수립과 조정
14. 정당해산의 제소
15. 정부에 제출 또는 회부된 정부의 정책에 관계되는 청원의 심사
16. 검찰총장·합동참모의장·각군참모총장·국립대학교총장·대사 기타 법률이 정한 공무원과 국영기업체관리자의 임명
17. 기타 대통령·국무총리 또는 국무위원이 제출한 사항

제90조 ①국정의 중요한 사항에 관한 대통령의 자문에 응하기 위하여 국가원로로 구성되는 국가원로자문회의를 둘 수 있다.

②국가원로자문회의의 의장은 직전대통령이 된다. 다만, 직전대통령이 없을 때에는 대통령이 지명한다.

③국가원로자문회의의 조직·직무범위 기타 필요한 사항은 법률로 정한다.

제91조 ①국가안전보장에 관련되는 대외정책·군사정책과 국내정책의 수립에 관하여 국무회의의 심의에 앞서 대통령의 자문에 응하기 위하여 국가안전보장회의를 둔다.

②국가안전보장회의는 대통령이 주재한다.

③국가안전보장회의의 조직·직무범위 기타 필요한 사항은 법률로 정한다.

제92조 ①평화통일정책의 수립에 관한 대통령의 자문에 응하기 위하여 민주평화통일자문회의를 둘 수 있다.

②민주평화통일자문회의의 조직·직무범위 기타 필요한 사항은 법률로 정한다.

제93조 ①국민경제의 발전을 위한 중요정책의 수립에 관하여 대통령의 자문에 응하기 위하여 국민경제자문회의를 둘 수 있다.

②국민경제자문회의의 조직·직무범위 기타 필요한 사항은 법률로 정한다.

제3관 행정각부

제94조 행정각부의 장은 국무위원 중에서 국무총리의 제청으로 대통령이 임명한다.

제95조 국무총리 또는 행정각부의 장은 소관사무에 관하여 법률이나 대통령령의 위임 또는 직권으로 총리령 또는 부령을 발할 수 있다.

제96조 행정각부의 설치·조직과 직무범위는 법률로 정한다.

제4관 감사원

제97조 국가의 세입·세출의 결산, 국가 및 법률이 정한 단체의 회계검사와 행정기관 및 공무원의 직무에 관한 감찰을 하기 위하여 대통령 소속하에 감사원을 둔다.

제98조 ①감사원은 원장을 포함한 5인 이상 11인 이하의 감사위원으로 구성한다.

②원장은 국회의 동의를 얻어 대통령이 임명하고, 그 임기는 4년으로 하며, 1차에 한하여 중임할 수 있다.

③감사위원은 원장의 제청으로 대통령이 임명하고, 그 임기는 4년으로 하며, 1차에 한하여 중임할 수 있다.

제99조 감사원은 세입·세출의 결산을 매년 검사하여 대통령과 차년도국회에 그 결과를 보고하여야 한다.

제100조 감사원의 조직·직무범위·감사위원의 자격·감사대상공무원의 범위 기타 필요한 사항은 법률로 정한다.

제 5 장 법 원

제101조 ①사법권은 법관으로 구성된 법원에 속한다.

②법원은 최고법원인 대법원과 각급법원으로 조직된다.

③법관의 자격은 법률로 정한다.

제102조 ①대법원에 부를 둘 수 있다.

②대법원에 대법관을 둔다. 다만, 법률이 정하는 바에 의하여 대법관이 아닌 법관을 둘 수 있다.

③대법원과 각급법원의 조직은 법률로 정한다.

제103조 법관은 헌법과 법률에 의하여 그 양심에 따라 독립하여 심판한다.

제104조 ①대법원장은 국회의 동의를 얻어 대통령이 임명한다.

②대법관은 대법원장의 제청으로 국회의 동의를 얻어 대통령이 임명한다.

③대법원장과 대법관이 아닌 법관은 대법관회의의 동의를 얻어 대법원장이 임명한다.

제105조 ①대법원장의 임기는 6년으로 하며, 중임할 수 없다.

②대법관의 임기는 6년으로 하며, 법률이 정하는 바에 의하여 연임할 수 있다.

③대법원장과 대법관이 아닌 법관의 임기는 10년으로 하며, 법률이 정하는 바에 의하여 연임할 수 있다.

④법관의 정년은 법률로 정한다.

제106조 ①법관은 탄핵 또는 금고 이상의 형의 선고에 의하지 아니하고는 파면되지 아니하며, 징계처분에 의하지 아니하고는 정직·감봉 기타 불리한 처분을 받지 아니한다.

②법관이 중대한 심신상의 장해로 직무를 수행할 수 없을 때에는 법률이 정하는 바에 의하여 퇴직하게 할 수 있다.

제107조 ①법률이 헌법에 위반되는 여부가 재판의 전제가 된 경우에는 법원은 헌법재판소에 제청하여 그 심판에 의하여 재판한다.

②명령·규칙 또는 처분이 헌법이나 법률에 위반되는 여부가 재판의 전제가 된

경우에는 대법원은 이를 최종적으로 심사할 권한을 가진다.

③재판의 전심절차로서 행정심판을 할 수 있다. 행정심판의 절차는 법률로 정하되, 사법절차가 준용되어야 한다.

제108조 대법원은 법률에 저촉되지 아니하는 범위 안에서 소송에 관한 절차, 법원의 내부규율과 사무처리에 관한 규칙을 제정할 수 있다.

제109조 재판의 심리와 판결은 공개한다. 다만, 심리는 국가의 안전보장 또는 안녕질서를 방해하거나 선량한 풍속을 해할 염려가 있을 때에는 법원의 결정으로 공개하지 아니할 수 있다.

제110조 ①군사재판을 관할하기 위하여 특별법원으로서 군사법원을 둘 수 있다.

②군사법원의 상고심은 대법원에서 관할한다.

③군사법원의 조직·권한 및 재판관의 자격은 법률로 정한다.

④비상계엄하의 군사재판은 군인·군무원의 범죄나 군사에 관한 간첩죄의 경우와 초병·초소·유독음식물공급·포로에 관한 죄 중 법률이 정한 경우에 한하여 단심으로 할 수 있다. 다만, 사형을 선고한 경우에는 그러하지 아니하다.

제 6 장 헌법재판소

제111조 ①헌법재판소는 다음 사항을 관장한다.

1. 법원의 제청에 의한 법률의 위헌여부 심판
2. 탄핵의 심판
3. 정당의 해산 심판
4. 국가기관 상호간, 국가기관과 지방자치단체간 및 지방자치단체 상호간의 권한쟁의에 관한 심판
5. 법률이 정하는 헌법소원에 관한 심판

②헌법재판소는 법관의 자격을 가진 9인의 재판관으로 구성하며, 재판관은 대통령이 임명한다.

③제2항의 재판관중 3인은 국회에서 선출하는 자를, 3인은 대법원장이 지명하는 자를 임명한다.

④헌법재판소의 장은 국회의 동의를 얻어 재판관 중에서 대통령이 임명한다.

제112조 ①헌법재판소 재판관의 임기는 6년으로 하며, 법률이 정하는 바에 의하

여 연임할 수 있다.

②헌법재판소 재판관은 정당에 가입하거나 정치에 관여할 수 없다.

③헌법재판소 재판관은 탄핵 또는 금고 이상의 형의 선고에 의하지 아니하고는 파면되지 아니한다.

제113조 ①헌법재판소에서 법률의 위헌결정, 탄핵의 결정, 정당해산의 결정 또는 헌법소원에 관한 인용결정을 할 때에는 재판관 6인 이상의 찬성이 있어야 한다.

②헌법재판소는 법률에 저촉되지 아니하는 범위 안에서 심판에 관한 절차, 내부규율과 사무처리에 관한 규칙을 제정할 수 있다.

③헌법재판소의 조직과 운영 기타 필요한 사항은 법률로 정한다.

제 7 장   선거관리

제114조 ①선거와 국민투표의 공정한 관리 및 정당에 관한 사무를 처리하기 위하여 선거관리위원회를 둔다.

②중앙선거관리위원회는 대통령이 임명하는 3인, 국회에서 선출하는 3인과 대법원장이 지명하는 3인의 위원으로 구성한다. 위원장은 위원 중에서 호선한다.

③위원의 임기는 6년으로 한다.

④위원은 정당에 가입하거나 정치에 관여할 수 없다.

⑤위원은 탄핵 또는 금고 이상의 형의 선고에 의하지 아니하고는 파면되지 아니한다.

⑥중앙선거관리위원회는 법령의 범위 안에서 선거관리·국민투표관리 또는 정당사무에 관한 규칙을 제정할 수 있으며, 법률에 저촉되지 아니하는 범위 안에서 내부규율에 관한 규칙을 제정할 수 있다.

⑦각급 선거관리위원회의 조직·직무범위 기타 필요한 사항은 법률로 정한다.

제115조 ①각급 선거관리위원회는 선거인명부의 작성 등 선거사무와 국민투표사무에 관하여 관계 행정기관에 필요한 지시를 할 수 있다.

②제1항의 지시를 받은 당해 행정기관은 이에 응하여야 한다.

제116조 ①선거운동은 각급 선거관리위원회의 관리하에 법률이 정하는 범위 안에서 하되, 균등한 기회가 보장되어야 한다.

②선거에 관한 경비는 법률이 정하는 경우를 제외하고는 정당 또는 후보자에게

부담시킬 수 없다.

제 8 장 지방자치

제117조 ①지방자치단체는 주민의 복리에 관한 사무를 처리하고 재산을 관리하며, 법령의 범위 안에서 자치에 관한 규정을 제정할 수 있다.
②지방자치단체의 종류는 법률로 정한다.

제118조 ①지방자치단체에 의회를 둔다.
②지방의회의 조직·권한·의원선거와 지방자치단체의 장의 선임방법 기타 지방자치단체의 조직과 운영에 관한 사항은 법률로 정한다.

제 9 장 경 제

제119조 ①대한민국의 경제질서는 개인과 기업의 경제상의 자유와 창의를 존중함을 기본으로 한다.
②국가는 균형있는 국민경제의 성장 및 안정과 적정한 소득의 분배를 유지하고, 시장의 지배와 경제력의 남용을 방지하며, 경제주체간의 조화를 통한 경제의 민주화를 위하여 경제에 관한 규제와 조정을 할 수 있다.

제120조 ①광물 기타 중요한 지하자원·수산자원·수력과 경제상 이용할 수 있는 자연력은 법률이 정하는 바에 의하여 일정한 기간 그 채취·개발 또는 이용을 특허할 수 있다.
②국토와 자원은 국가의 보호를 받으며, 국가는 그 균형있는 개발과 이용을 위하여 필요한 계획을 수립한다.

제121조 ①국가는 농지에 관하여 경자유전의 원칙이 달성될 수 있도록 노력하여야 하며, 농지의 소작제도는 금지된다.
②농업생산성의 제고와 농지의 합리적인 이용을 위하거나 불가피한 사정으로 발생하는 농지의 임대차와 위탁경영은 법률이 정하는 바에 의하여 인정된다.

제122조 국가는 국민 모두의 생산 및 생활의 기반이 되는 국토의 효율적이고 균형있는 이용·개발과 보전을 위하여 법률이 정하는 바에 의하여 그에 관한 필요한

제한과 의무를 과할 수 있다.

제123조 ①국가는 농업 및 어업을 보호·육성하기 위하여 농·어촌종합개발과 그 지원등 필요한 계획을 수립·시행하여야 한다.

②국가는 지역간의 균형있는 발전을 위하여 지역경제를 육성할 의무를 진다.

③국가는 중소기업을 보호·육성하여야 한다.

④국가는 농수산물의 수급균형과 유통구조의 개선에 노력하여 가격안정을 도모함으로써 농·어민의 이익을 보호한다.

⑤국가는 농·어민과 중소기업의 자조조직을 육성하여야 하며, 그 자율적 활동과 발전을 보장한다.

제124조 국가는 건전한 소비행위를 계도하고 생산품의 품질향상을 촉구하기 위한 소비자보호운동을 법률이 정하는 바에 의하여 보장한다.

제125조 국가는 대외무역을 육성하며, 이를 규제·조정할 수 있다.

제126조 국방상 또는 국민경제상 긴절한 필요로 인하여 법률이 정하는 경우를 제외하고는, 사영기업을 국유 또는 공유로 이전하거나 그 경영을 통제 또는 관리할 수 없다.

제127조 ①국가는 과학기술의 혁신과 정보 및 인력의 개발을 통하여 국민경제의 발전에 노력하여야 한다.

②국가는 국가표준제도를 확립한다.

③대통령은 제1항의 목적을 달성하기 위하여 필요한 자문기구를 둘 수 있다.

제 10 장   헌법개정

제128조 ①헌법개정은 국회재적의원 과반수 또는 대통령의 발의로 제안된다.

②대통령의 임기연장 또는 중임변경을 위한 헌법개정은 그 헌법개정 제안 당시의 대통령에 대하여는 효력이 없다.

제129조 제안된 헌법개정안은 대통령이 20일 이상의 기간 이를 공고하여야 한다.

제130조 ①국회는 헌법개정안이 공고된 날로부터 60일 이내에 의결하여야 하며, 국회의 의결은 재적의원 3분의 2 이상의 찬성을 얻어야 한다.

②헌법개정안은 국회가 의결한 후 30일 이내에 국민투표에 붙여 국회의원선거권자 과반수의 투표와 투표자 과반수의 찬성을 얻어야 한다.

③헌법개정안이 제2항의 찬성을 얻은 때에는 헌법개정은 확정되며, 대통령은 즉시 이를 공포하여야 한다.

부칙 〈제10호, 1987. 10. 29.〉

제1조 이 헌법은 1988년 2월 25일부터 시행한다. 다만, 이 헌법을 시행하기 위하여 필요한 법률의 제정·개정과 이 헌법에 의한 대통령 및 국회의원의 선거 기타 이 헌법시행에 관한 준비는 이 헌법시행 전에 할 수 있다.

제2조 ①이 헌법에 의한 최초의 대통령선거는 이 헌법시행일 40일 전까지 실시한다.

②이 헌법에 의한 최초의 대통령의 임기는 이 헌법시행일로부터 개시한다.

제3조 ①이 헌법에 의한 최초의 국회의원선거는 이 헌법공포일로부터 6월 이내에 실시하며, 이 헌법에 의하여 선출된 최초의 국회의원의 임기는 국회의원선거 후 이 헌법에 의한 국회의 최초의 집회일로부터 개시한다.

②이 헌법공포 당시의 국회의원의 임기는 제1항에 의한 국회의 최초의 집회일 전일까지로 한다.

제4조 ①이 헌법시행 당시의 공무원과 정부가 임명한 기업체의 임원은 이 헌법에 의하여 임명된 것으로 본다. 다만, 이 헌법에 의하여 선임방법이나 임명권자가 변경된 공무원과 대법원장 및 감사원장은 이 헌법에 의하여 후임자가 선임될 때까지 그 직무를 행하며, 이 경우 전임자인 공무원의 임기는 후임자가 선임되는 전일까지로 한다.

②이 헌법시행 당시의 대법원장과 대법원판사가 아닌 법관은 제1항 단서의 규정에 불구하고 이 헌법에 의하여 임명된 것으로 본다.

③이 헌법 중 공무원의 임기 또는 중임제한에 관한 규정은 이 헌법에 의하여 그 공무원이 최초로 선출 또는 임명된 때로부터 적용한다.

제5조 이 헌법시행 당시의 법령과 조약은 이 헌법에 위배되지 아니하는 한 그 효력을 지속한다.

제6조 이 헌법시행 당시에 이 헌법에 의하여 새로 설치될 기관의 권한에 속하는 직무를 행하고 있는 기관은 이 헌법에 의하여 새로운 기관이 설치될 때까지 존속하며 그 직무를 행한다.

The Constitution of the United States

Preamble

We the People of the United States, in Order to form a more perfect Union, establish Justice, insure domestic Tranquility, provide for the common defence, promote the general Welfare, and secure the Blessings of Liberty to ourselves and our Posterity, do ordain and establish this Constitution for the United States of America.

Article. I. - The Legislative Branch

Section 1 - The Legislature

All legislative Powers herein granted shall be vested in a Congress of the United States, which shall consist of a Senate and House of Representatives.

Section 2 - The House

The House of Representatives shall be composed of Members chosen every second Year by the People of the several States, and the Electors in each State shall have the Qualifications requisite for Electors of the most numerous Branch of the State Legislature.

No Person shall be a Representative who shall not have attained to the Age of twenty five Years, and been seven Years a Citizen of the United States, and who shall not, when elected, be an Inhabitant of that State in which he shall be chosen.

(Representatives and direct Taxes shall be apportioned among the several States which may be included within this Union, according to their respective Numbers, which shall be determined by adding to the whole Number of free Persons, including those bound to Service for a Term of Years, and excluding Indians not taxed, three fifths of all other Persons.) **(The previous sentence in parentheses was modified by the 14th Amendment, section 2.)** The actual Enumeration shall be made within three Years after the first Meeting of the Congress of the United States, and within every subsequent Term of ten Years, in such Manner as they shall by Law direct. The Number of Representatives shall not exceed one for every thirty Thousand, but each State shall have at Least one Representative; and until such enumeration shall be made, the State of New Hampshire shall be entitled to chuse three, Massachusetts eight, Rhode Island and Providence Plantations one, Connecticut five, New York six, New Jersey four, Pennsylvania eight, Delaware one, Maryland six, Virginia ten, North Carolina five, South Carolina five and Georgia three.

When vacancies happen in the Representation from any State, the Executive Authority thereof shall issue Writs of Election to fill such Vacancies.

The House of Representatives shall chuse their Speaker and other Officers; and shall have the sole Power of Impeachment.

Section 3 - The Senate

The Senate of the United States shall be composed of two Senators from each State, *(chosen by the Legislature thereof,)* **(The preceding words in parentheses superseded by 17th Amendment, section 1.)** for six Years; and each Senator shall have one Vote.

Immediately after they shall be assembled in Consequence of the first Election, they shall be divided as equally as may be into three Classes. The Seats of the Senators of the first Class shall be vacated at the Expiration of the second Year, of the second Class at the Expiration of the fourth Year, and of the third Class at the Expiration of the sixth Year, so that one third may be chosen every second Year; *(and if Vacancies happen by Resignation, or otherwise, during the Recess of the Legislature of any State, the Executive thereof may make temporary Appointments until the next Meeting of the Legislature, which shall then fill such Vacancies.)* **(The preceding words in parentheses were superseded by the 17th Amendment, section 2.)**

No person shall be a Senator who shall not have attained to the Age of thirty Years, and been nine Years a Citizen of the United States, and who shall not, when elected, be an Inhabitant of that State for which he shall be chosen.

The Vice President of the United States shall be President of the Senate, but shall have no Vote, unless they be equally divided.

The Senate shall chuse their other Officers, and also a President pro tempore, in the absence of the Vice President, or when he shall exercise the Office of President of the United States.

The Senate shall have the sole Power to try all Impeachments. When sitting for that Purpose, they shall be on Oath or Affirmation. When the President of the United States is tried, the Chief Justice shall preside: And no Person shall be convicted without the Concurrence of two thirds of the Members present.

Judgment in Cases of Impeachment shall not extend further than to removal from Office, and disqualification to hold and enjoy any Office of honor, Trust or Profit under the United States: but the Party convicted shall nevertheless be liable and subject to Indictment, Trial, Judgment and Punishment, according to Law.

Section 4 - Elections, Meetings

The Times, Places and Manner of holding Elections for Senators and Representatives, shall be prescribed in each State by the Legislature thereof; but the Congress may at any time by Law make or alter such Regulations, except as to the Place of Chusing Senators.

The Congress shall assemble at least once in every Year, and such Meeting shall *(be on the first Monday in December,)* **(The preceding words in parentheses were superseded by the 20th Amendment, section 2.)** unless they shall by Law appoint a different Day.

Section 5 - Membership, Rules, Journals, Adjournment

Each House shall be the Judge of the Elections, Returns and Qualifications of its own Members, and a Majority of each shall constitute a Quorum to do Business; but a smaller number may adjourn from day to day, and may be authorized to compel the Attendance of absent Members, in such Manner, and under such Penalties as each House may provide.

Each House may determine the Rules of its Proceedings, punish its Members for disorderly Behavior, and, with the Concurrence of two-thirds, expel a Member.

Each House shall keep a Journal of its Proceedings, and from time to time publish the same, excepting such Parts as may in their Judgment require Secrecy; and the Yeas and Nays of the Members of either House on any question shall, at the Desire of one fifth of those Present, be entered on the Journal.

Neither House, during the Session of Congress, shall, without the Consent of the other, adjourn for more than three days, nor to any other Place than that in which the two Houses shall be sitting.

Section 6 - Compensation

(The Senators and Representatives shall receive a Compensation for their Services, to be ascertained by Law, and paid out of the Treasury of the United States.) **(The preceding words in parentheses were modified by the 27th Amendment.)** They shall in all Cases, except Treason, Felony and Breach of the Peace, be privileged from Arrest during their Attendance at the Session of their respective Houses, and in going to and returning from the same; and for any Speech or Debate in either House, they shall not be questioned in any other Place.

No Senator or Representative shall, during the Time for which he was elected, be appointed to any civil Office under the Authority of the United States which shall have been created, or the Emoluments whereof shall have been increased during such time; and no Person holding any Office under the United States, shall be a Member of either House during his Continuance in Office.

Section 7 - Revenue Bills, Legislative Process, Presidential Veto

All bills for raising Revenue shall originate in the House of Representatives; but the Senate may propose or concur with Amendments as on other Bills.

Every Bill which shall have passed the House of Representatives and the Senate, shall, before it become a Law, be presented to the President of the United States; If he approve he shall sign it, but if not he shall return it, with his Objections to that House in which it shall have originated, who shall enter the Objections at large on their Journal, and proceed to reconsider it. If after such Reconsideration two thirds of that House shall agree to pass the Bill, it shall be sent, together with the Objections, to the other House, by which it shall likewise be reconsidered, and if approved by two thirds of that House, it shall become a Law. But in all such Cases the Votes of both Houses shall be determined by Yeas and Nays, and the Names of the Persons voting for and against the Bill shall be entered on the Journal of each House respectively. If any Bill shall not be returned by the President within ten Days (Sundays excepted) after it shall have been presented to him, the Same shall be a Law, in like Manner as if he had signed it, unless the Congress by their Adjournment prevent its Return, in which Case it shall not be a Law.

Every Order, Resolution, or Vote to which the Concurrence of the Senate and House of Representatives may be necessary (except on a question of Adjournment) shall be presented to the President of the United States; and before the Same shall take Effect, shall be approved by him, or being disapproved by him, shall be repassed by two thirds of the Senate and House of Representatives, according to the Rules and Limitations prescribed in the Case of a Bill.

Section 8 - Powers of Congress

The Congress shall have Power To lay and collect Taxes, Duties, Imposts and Excises, to pay the Debts and provide for the common Defence and general Welfare of the United States; but all Duties, Imposts and Excises shall be uniform throughout the United States;

To borrow money on the credit of the United States;

To regulate Commerce with foreign Nations, and among the several States, and with the Indian Tribes;

To establish an uniform Rule of Naturalization, and uniform Laws on the subject of Bankruptcies throughout the United States;

To coin Money, regulate the Value thereof, and of foreign Coin, and fix the Standard of Weights and Measures;

To provide for the Punishment of counterfeiting the Securities and current Coin of the United States;

To establish Post Offices and Post Roads;

To promote the Progress of Science and useful Arts, by securing for limited Times to Authors and Inventors the exclusive Right to their respective Writings and Discoveries;

To constitute Tribunals inferior to the supreme Court;

To define and punish Piracies and Felonies committed on the high Seas, and Offenses against the Law of Nations;

To declare War, grant Letters of Marque and Reprisal, and make Rules concerning Captures on Land and Water;

To raise and support Armies, but no Appropriation of Money to that Use shall be for a longer Term than two Years;

To provide and maintain a Navy;

To make Rules for the Government and Regulation of the land and naval Forces;

To provide for calling forth the Militia to execute the Laws of the Union, suppress Insurrections and repel Invasions;

To provide for organizing, arming, and disciplining the Militia, and for governing such Part of them as may be employed in the Service of the United States, reserving to the States respectively, the Appointment of the Officers, and the Authority of training the Militia according to the discipline prescribed by Congress;

To exercise exclusive Legislation in all Cases whatsoever, over such District (not exceeding ten Miles square) as may, by Cession of particular States, and the acceptance of Congress, become the Seat of the Government of the United States, and to exercise like Authority over all Places purchased by the Consent of the Legislature of the State in which the Same shall be, for the Erection of Forts, Magazines, Arsenals, dock-Yards, and other needful Buildings; And

To make all Laws which shall be necessary and proper for carrying into Execution the foregoing Powers, and all other Powers vested by this Constitution in the Government of the United States, or in any Department or Officer thereof.

Section 9 - Limits on Congress

The Migration or Importation of such Persons as any of the States now existing shall think proper to admit, shall not be prohibited by the Congress prior to the Year one thousand eight hundred and eight, but a tax or duty may be imposed on such Importation, not exceeding ten dollars for each Person.

The privilege of the Writ of Habeas Corpus shall not be suspended, unless when in Cases of Rebellion or Invasion the public Safety may require it.

No Bill of Attainder or ex post facto Law shall be passed.

(No capitation, or other direct, Tax shall be laid, unless in Proportion to the Census or Enumeration herein before directed to be taken.) **(Section in parentheses clarified by the 16th Amendment.)**

No Tax or Duty shall be laid on Articles exported from any State.

No Preference shall be given by any Regulation of Commerce or Revenue to the Ports of one State over those of another: nor shall Vessels bound to, or from, one State, be obliged to enter, clear, or pay Duties in another.

No Money shall be drawn from the Treasury, but in Consequence of Appropriations made by Law; and a regular Statement and Account of the Receipts and Expenditures of all public Money shall be published from time to time.

No Title of Nobility shall be granted by the United States: And no Person holding any Office of Profit or Trust under them, shall, without the Consent of the Congress, accept of any present, Emolument, Office, or Title, of any kind whatever, from any King, Prince or foreign State.

Section 10 - Powers prohibited of States

No State shall enter into any Treaty, Alliance, or Confederation; grant Letters of Marque and Reprisal; coin Money; emit Bills of Credit; make any Thing but gold and silver Coin a Tender in Payment of Debts; pass any Bill of Attainder, ex post facto Law, or Law impairing the Obligation of Contracts, or grant any Title of Nobility.

No State shall, without the Consent of the Congress, lay any Imposts or Duties on Imports or Exports, except what may be absolutely necessary for executing it's inspection Laws: and the net Produce of all Duties and Imposts, laid by any State on Imports or Exports, shall be for the Use of the Treasury of the United States; and all such Laws shall be subject to the Revision and Controul of the Congress.

No State shall, without the Consent of Congress, lay any duty of Tonnage, keep Troops, or Ships of War in time of Peace, enter into any Agreement or Compact with another State, or with a foreign Power, or engage in War, unless actually invaded, or in such imminent Danger as will not admit of delay.

Article. II. - The Executive Branch

Section 1 - The President

The executive Power shall be vested in a President of the United States of America. He shall hold his Office during the Term of four Years, and, together with the Vice-President chosen for the same Term, be elected, as follows:

Each State shall appoint, in such Manner as the Legislature thereof may direct, a Number of Electors, equal to the whole Number of Senators and Representatives to which the State may be entitled in the Congress: but no Senator or Representative, or Person holding an Office of Trust or Profit under the United States, shall be appointed an Elector.

(The Electors shall meet in their respective States, and vote by Ballot for two persons, of whom one at least shall not lie an Inhabitant of the same State with themselves. And they shall make a List of all the Persons voted for, and of the Number of Votes for each; which List they shall sign and certify, and transmit sealed to the Seat of the Government of the United States, directed to the President of the Senate. The President of the Senate shall, in the Presence of the Senate and House of Representatives, open all the Certificates, and the Votes shall then be counted. The Person having the greatest Number of Votes shall be the President, if such Number be a Majority of the whole Number of Electors appointed; and if there be more than one who have such Majority, and have an equal Number of Votes, then the House of Representatives shall immediately chuse by Ballot one of them for President; and if no Person have a Majority, then from the five highest on the List the said House shall in like Manner chuse the President. But in chusing the President, the Votes shall be taken by States, the Representation from each State having one Vote; a quorum for this Purpose shall consist of a Member or Members from two-thirds of the States, and a Majority of all the States shall be necessary to a Choice. In every Case, after the Choice of the President, the Person having the greatest Number of Votes of the Electors shall be the Vice President. But if there should remain two or more who have equal Votes, the Senate shall chuse from them by Ballot the Vice-President.) **(This clause in parentheses was superseded by the 12th Amendment.)**

The Congress may determine the Time of chusing the Electors, and the Day on which they shall give their Votes; which Day shall be the same throughout the United States.

No person except a natural born Citizen, or a Citizen of the United States, at the time of the Adoption of this Constitution, shall be eligible to the Office of President; neither shall any Person be eligible to that Office who shall not have attained to the Age of thirty-five Years, and been fourteen Years a Resident within the United States.

(In Case of the Removal of the President from Office, or of his Death, Resignation, or Inability to discharge the Powers and Duties of the said Office, the same shall devolve on the Vice President, and the Congress may by Law provide for the Case of Removal, Death, Resignation or Inability, both of the President and Vice President, declaring what Officer shall then act as President, and such Officer shall act accordingly, until the Disability be removed, or a President shall be elected.) **(This clause in parentheses has been modified by the 20th and 25th Amendments.)**

The President shall, at stated Times, receive for his Services, a Compensation, which shall neither be increased nor diminished during the Period for which he shall have been elected, and he shall not receive within that Period any other Emolument from the United States, or any of them.

Before he enter on the Execution of his Office, he shall take the following Oath or Affirmation:

"I do solemnly swear (or affirm) that I will faithfully execute the Office of President of the United States, and will to the best of my Ability, preserve, protect and defend the Constitution of the United States."

Section 2 - Civilian Power over Military, Cabinet, Pardon Power, Appointments

The President shall be Commander in Chief of the Army and Navy of the United States, and of the Militia of the several States, when called into the actual Service of the United States; he may require the Opinion, in writing, of the principal Officer in each of the executive Departments, upon any subject relating to the Duties of their respective Offices, and he shall have Power to Grant Reprieves and Pardons for Offenses against the United States, except in Cases of Impeachment.

He shall have Power, by and with the Advice and Consent of the Senate, to make Treaties, provided two thirds of the Senators present concur; and he shall nominate, and by and with the Advice and Consent of the Senate, shall appoint Ambassadors, other public Ministers and Consuls, Judges of the supreme Court, and all other Officers of the United States, whose Appointments are not herein otherwise provided for, and which shall be established by Law: but the Congress may by Law vest the Appointment of such inferior Officers, as they think proper, in the President alone, in the Courts of Law, or in the Heads of Departments.

The President shall have Power to fill up all Vacancies that may happen during the Recess of the Senate, by granting Commissions which shall expire at the End of their next Session.

Section 3 - State of the Union, Convening Congress

He shall from time to time give to the Congress Information of the State of the Union, and recommend to their Consideration such Measures as he shall judge necessary and expedient; he may, on extraordinary Occasions, convene both Houses, or either of them, and in Case of Disagreement between them, with Respect to the Time of Adjournment, he may adjourn them to such Time as he shall think proper; he shall receive Ambassadors and other public Ministers; he shall take Care that the Laws be faithfully executed, and shall Commission all the Officers of the United States.

Section 4 - Disqualification

The President, Vice President and all civil Officers of the United States, shall be removed from Office on Impeachment for, and Conviction of, Treason, Bribery, or other high Crimes and Misdemeanors.

Article III. - The Judicial Branch

Section 1 - Judicial powers

The judicial Power of the United States, shall be vested in one supreme Court, and in such inferior Courts as the Congress may from time to time ordain and establish. The Judges, both of the supreme and inferior Courts, shall hold their Offices during good Behavior, and shall, at stated Times, receive for their Services a Compensation which shall not be diminished during their Continuance in Office.

Section 2 - Trial by Jury, Original Jurisdiction, Jury Trials

(The judicial Power shall extend to all Cases, in Law and Equity, arising under this Constitution, the Laws of the United States, and Treaties made, or which shall be made, under their Authority; to all Cases affecting Ambassadors, other public Ministers and Consuls; to all Cases of admiralty and maritime Jurisdiction; to Controversies to which the United States shall be a Party; to Controversies between two or more States; between a State and Citizens of another State; between Citizens of different States; between Citizens of the same State claiming Lands under Grants of different States, and between a State, or the Citizens thereof, and foreign States, Citizens or Subjects.) **(This section in parentheses is modified by the 11th Amendment.)**

In all Cases affecting Ambassadors, other public Ministers and Consuls, and those in which a State shall be Party, the supreme Court shall have original Jurisdiction. In all the other Cases before mentioned, the supreme Court shall have appellate Jurisdiction, both as to Law and Fact, with such Exceptions, and under such Regulations as the Congress shall make.

The Trial of all Crimes, except in Cases of Impeachment, shall be by Jury; and such Trial shall be held in the State where the said Crimes shall have been committed; but when not committed within any State, the Trial shall be at such Place or Places as the Congress may by Law have directed.

Section 3 - Treason

Treason against the United States, shall consist only in levying War against them, or in adhering to their Enemies, giving them Aid and Comfort. No Person shall be convicted of Treason unless on the Testimony of two Witnesses to the same overt Act, or on Confession in open Court.

The Congress shall have power to declare the Punishment of Treason, but no Attainder of Treason shall work Corruption of Blood, or Forfeiture except during the Life of the Person attainted.

Article. IV. - The States

Section 1 - Each State to Honor all others

Full Faith and Credit shall be given in each State to the public Acts, Records, and judicial Proceedings of every other State. And the Congress may by general Laws prescribe the Manner in which such Acts, Records and Proceedings shall be proved, and the Effect thereof.

Section 2 - State citizens, Extradition

The Citizens of each State shall be entitled to all Privileges and Immunities of Citizens in the several States.

A Person charged in any State with Treason, Felony, or other Crime, who shall flee from Justice, and be found in another State, shall on demand of the executive Authority of the State from which he fled, be delivered up, to be removed to the State having Jurisdiction of the Crime.

(No Person held to Service or Labour in one State, under the Laws thereof, escaping into another, shall, in Consequence of any Law or Regulation therein, be discharged from such Service or Labour, But shall be delivered up on Claim of the Party to whom such Service or Labour may be due.) **(This clause in parentheses is superseded by the 13th Amendment.)**

Section 3 - New States

New States may be admitted by the Congress into this Union; but no new States shall be formed or erected within the Jurisdiction of any other State; nor any State be formed by the Junction of two or more States, or parts of States, without the Consent of the Legislatures of the States concerned as well as of the Congress.

The Congress shall have Power to dispose of and make all needful Rules and Regulations respecting the Territory or other Property belonging to the United States; and nothing in this Constitution shall be so construed as to Prejudice any Claims of the United States, or of any particular State.

Section 4 - Republican government

The United States shall guarantee to every State in this Union a Republican Form of Government, and shall protect each of them against Invasion; and on Application of the Legislature, or of the Executive (when the Legislature cannot be convened) against domestic Violence.

Article. V. - Amendment

The Congress, whenever two thirds of both Houses shall deem it necessary, shall propose Amendments to this Constitution, or, on the Application of the Legislatures of two thirds of the several States, shall call a Convention for proposing Amendments, which, in either Case, shall be valid to all Intents and Purposes, as part of this Constitution, when ratified by the Legislatures of three fourths of the several States, or by Conventions in three fourths thereof, as the one or the other Mode of Ratification may be proposed by the Congress; Provided that no Amendment which may be made prior to the Year One thousand eight hundred and eight shall in any Manner affect the first and fourth Clauses in the Ninth Section of the first Article; and that no State, without its Consent, shall be deprived of its equal Suffrage in the Senate.

Article. VI. - Debts, Supremacy, Oaths

All Debts contracted and Engagements entered into, before the Adoption of this Constitution, shall be as valid against the United States under this Constitution, as under the Confederation.

This Constitution, and the Laws of the United States which shall be made in Pursuance thereof; and all Treaties made, or which shall be made, under the Authority of the United States, shall be the supreme Law of the Land; and the Judges in every State shall be bound thereby, any Thing in the Constitution or Laws of any State to the Contrary notwithstanding.

The Senators and Representatives before mentioned, and the Members of the several State Legislatures, and all executive and judicial Officers, both of the United States and of the several States, shall be bound by Oath or Affirmation, to support this Constitution; but no religious Test shall ever be required as a Qualification to any Office or public Trust under the United States.

Article. VII. - Ratification

The Ratification of the Conventions of nine States, shall be sufficient for the Establishment of this Constitution between the States so ratifying the Same.

Done in Convention by the Unanimous Consent of the States present the Seventeenth Day of September in the Year of our Lord one thousand seven hundred and Eighty seven and of the Independence of the United States of America the Twelfth. In Witness whereof We have hereunto subscribed our Names.

Go Washington - President and deputy from Virginia

New Hampshire - John Langdon, Nicholas Gilman

Massachusetts - Nathaniel Gorham, Rufus King

Connecticut - Wm Saml Johnson, Roger Sherman

New York - Alexander Hamilton

New Jersey - Wil Livingston, David Brearley, Wm Paterson, Jona. Dayton

Pensylvania - B Franklin, Thomas Mifflin, Robt Morris, Geo. Clymer, Thos FitzSimons, Jared Ingersoll, James Wilson, Gouv Morris

Delaware - Geo. Read, Gunning Bedford jun, John Dickinson, Richard Bassett, Jaco. Broom

Maryland - James McHenry, Dan of St Tho Jenifer, Danl Carroll

Virginia - John Blair, James Madison Jr.

North Carolina - Wm Blount, Richd Dobbs Spaight, Hu Williamson

South Carolina - J. Rutledge, Charles Cotesworth Pinckney, Charles Pinckney, Pierce Butler

Georgia - William Few, Abr Baldwin

Attest: William Jackson, Secretary

The Amendments

The following are the Amendments to the Constitution. The first ten Amendments collectively are commonly known as the Bill of Rights.

Amendment 1 - Freedom of Religion, Press, Expression. Ratified 12/15/1791.

Congress shall make no law respecting an establishment of religion, or prohibiting the free exercise thereof; or abridging the freedom of speech, or of the press; or the right of the people peaceably to assemble, and to petition the Government for a redress of grievances.

Amendment 2 - Right to Bear Arms. Ratified 12/15/1791.

A well regulated Militia, being necessary to the security of a free State, the right of the people to keep and bear Arms, shall not be infringed.

Amendment 3 - Quartering of Soldiers. Ratified 12/15/1791.

No Soldier shall, in time of peace be quartered in any house, without the consent of the Owner, nor in time of war, but in a manner to be prescribed by law.

Amendment 4 - Search and Seizure. Ratified 12/15/1791.

The right of the people to be secure in their persons, houses, papers, and effects, against unreasonable searches and seizures, shall not be violated, and no Warrants shall issue, but upon probable cause, supported by Oath or affirmation, and particularly describing the place to be searched, and the persons or things to be seized.

Amendment 5 - Trial and Punishment, Compensation for Takings. Ratified 12/15/1791.

No person shall be held to answer for a capital, or otherwise infamous crime, unless on a presentment or indictment of a Grand Jury, except in cases arising in the land or naval forces, or in the Militia, when in actual service in time of War or public danger; nor shall any person be subject for the same offense to be twice put in jeopardy of life or limb; nor shall be compelled in any criminal case to be a witness against himself, nor be deprived of life, liberty, or property, without due process of law; nor shall private property be taken for public use, without just compensation.

Amendment 6 - Right to Speedy Trial, Confrontation of Witnesses. Ratified 12/15/1791.

In all criminal prosecutions, the accused shall enjoy the right to a speedy and public trial, by an impartial jury of the State and district wherein the crime shall have been committed, which district shall have been previously ascertained by law, and to be informed of the nature and cause of the accusation; to be confronted with the witnesses against him; to have compulsory process for obtaining witnesses in his favor, and to have the Assistance of Counsel for his defence.

Amendment 7 - Trial by Jury in Civil Cases. Ratified 12/15/1791.

In Suits at common law, where the value in controversy shall exceed twenty dollars, the right of trial by jury shall be preserved, and no fact tried by a jury, shall be otherwise re-examined in any Court of the United States, than according to the rules of the common law.

Amendment 8 - Cruel and Unusual Punishment. Ratified 12/15/1791.

Excessive bail shall not be required, nor excessive fines imposed, nor cruel and unusual punishments inflicted.

Amendment 9 - Construction of Constitution. Ratified 12/15/1791.

The enumeration in the Constitution, of certain rights, shall not be construed to deny or disparage others retained by the people.

Amendment 10 - Powers of the States and People. Ratified 12/15/1791.

The powers not delegated to the United States by the Constitution, nor prohibited by it to the States, are reserved to the States respectively, or to the people.

Amendment 11 - Judicial Limits. Ratified 2/7/1795.

The Judicial power of the United States shall not be construed to extend to any suit in law or equity, commenced or prosecuted against one of the United States by Citizens of another State, or by Citizens or Subjects of any Foreign State.

Amendment 12 - Choosing the President, Vice-President. Ratified 6/15/1804.

The Electors shall meet in their respective states, and vote by ballot for President and Vice-President, one of whom, at least, shall not be an inhabitant of the same state with themselves; they shall name in their ballots the person voted for as President, and in distinct ballots the person voted for as Vice-President, and they shall make distinct lists of all persons voted for as President, and of all persons voted for as Vice-President and of the number of votes for each, which lists they shall sign and certify, and transmit sealed to the seat of the government of the United States, directed to the President of the Senate;

The President of the Senate shall, in the presence of the Senate and House of Representatives, open all the certificates and the votes shall then be counted;

The person having the greatest Number of votes for President, shall be the President, if such number be a majority of the whole number of Electors appointed; and if no person have such majority, then from the persons having the highest numbers not exceeding three on the list of those voted for as President, the House of Representatives shall choose immediately, by ballot, the President. But in choosing the President, the votes shall be taken by states, the representation from each state having one vote; a quorum for this purpose shall consist of a member or members from two-thirds of the states, and a majority of all the states shall be necessary to a choice. And if the House of Representatives shall not choose a President whenever the right of choice shall devolve upon them, before the fourth day of March next following, then the Vice-President shall act as President, as in the case of the death or other constitutional disability of the President.

The person having the greatest number of votes as Vice-President, shall be the Vice-President, if such number be a majority of the whole number of Electors appointed, and if no person have a majority, then from the two highest numbers on the list, the Senate shall choose the Vice-President; a quorum for the purpose shall consist of two-thirds of the whole number of Senators, and a majority of the whole number shall be necessary to a choice. But no person constitutionally ineligible to the office of President shall be eligible to that of Vice-President of the United States.

Amendment 13 - Slavery Abolished. Ratified 12/6/1865.

1. Neither slavery nor involuntary servitude, except as a punishment for crime whereof the party shall have been duly convicted, shall exist within the United States, or any place subject to their jurisdiction.

2. Congress shall have power to enforce this article by appropriate legislation.

Amendment 14 - Citizenship Rights. Ratified 7/9/1868.

1. All persons born or naturalized in the United States, and subject to the jurisdiction thereof, are citizens of the United States and of the State wherein they reside. No State shall make or enforce any law which shall abridge the privileges or immunities of citizens of the United States; nor shall any State deprive any person of life, liberty, or property, without due process of law; nor deny to any person within its jurisdiction the equal protection of the laws.

2. Representatives shall be apportioned among the several States according to their respective numbers, counting the whole number of persons in each State, excluding Indians not taxed. But when the right to vote at any election for the choice of electors for President and Vice-President of the United States, Representatives in Congress, the Executive and Judicial officers of a State, or the members of the Legislature thereof, is denied to any of the male inhabitants of such State, being twenty-one years of age, and citizens of the United States, or in any way abridged, except for participation in rebellion, or other crime, the basis of representation therein shall be reduced in the proportion which the number of such male citizens shall bear to the whole number of male citizens twenty-one years of age in such State.

3. No person shall be a Senator or Representative in Congress, or elector of President and Vice-President, or hold any office, civil or military, under the United States, or under any State, who, having previously taken an oath, as a member of Congress, or as an officer of the United States, or as a member of any State legislature, or as an executive or judicial officer of any State, to support the Constitution of the United States, shall have engaged in insurrection or rebellion against the same, or given aid or comfort to the enemies thereof. But Congress may by a vote of two-thirds of each House, remove such disability.

4. The validity of the public debt of the United States, authorized by law, including debts incurred for payment of pensions and bounties for services in suppressing insurrection or rebellion, shall not be questioned. But neither the United States nor any State shall assume or pay any debt or obligation incurred in aid of insurrection or rebellion against the United States, or any claim for the loss or emancipation of any slave; but all such debts, obligations and claims shall be held illegal and void.

5. The Congress shall have power to enforce, by appropriate legislation, the provisions of this article.

Amendment 15 - Race No Bar to Vote. Ratified 2/3/1870.

1. The right of citizens of the United States to vote shall not be denied or abridged by the United States or by any State on account of race, color, or previous condition of servitude.

2. The Congress shall have power to enforce this article by appropriate legislation.

Amendment 16 - Status of Income Tax Clarified. Ratified 2/3/1913.

The Congress shall have power to lay and collect taxes on incomes, from whatever source derived, without apportionment among the several States, and without regard to any census or enumeration.

Amendment 17 - Senators Elected by Popular Vote. Ratified 4/8/1913.

The Senate of the United States shall be composed of two Senators from each State, elected by the people thereof, for six years; and each Senator shall have one vote. The electors in each State shall have the qualifications requisite for electors of the most numerous branch of the State legislatures.

When vacancies happen in the representation of any State in the Senate, the executive authority of such State shall issue writs of election to fill such vacancies: Provided, That the legislature of any State may empower the executive thereof to make temporary appointments until the people fill the vacancies by election as the legislature may direct.

This amendment shall not be so construed as to affect the election or term of any Senator chosen before it becomes valid as part of the Constitution.

Amendment 18 - Liquor Abolished. Ratified 1/16/1919. Repealed by Amendment 21, 12/5/1933.

1. After one year from the ratification of this article the manufacture, sale, or transportation of intoxicating liquors within, the importation thereof into, or the exportation thereof from the United States and all territory subject to the jurisdiction thereof for beverage purposes is hereby prohibited.

2. The Congress and the several States shall have concurrent power to enforce this article by appropriate legislation.

3. This article shall be inoperative unless it shall have been ratified as an amendment to the Constitution by the legislatures of the several States, as provided in the Constitution, within seven years from the date of the submission hereof to the States by the Congress.

Amendment 19 - Women's Suffrage. Ratified 8/18/1920.

The right of citizens of the United States to vote shall not be denied or abridged by the United States or by any State on account of sex.

Congress shall have power to enforce this article by appropriate legislation.

Amendment 20 - Presidential, Congressional Terms. Ratified 1/23/1933.

1. The terms of the President and Vice President shall end at noon on the 20th day of January, and the terms of Senators and Representatives at noon on the 3d day of January, of the years in which such terms would have ended if this article had not been ratified; and the terms of their successors shall then begin.

2. The Congress shall assemble at least once in every year, and such meeting shall begin at noon on the 3d day of January, unless they shall by law appoint a different day.

3. If, at the time fixed for the beginning of the term of the President, the President elect shall have died, the Vice President elect shall become President. If a President shall not have been chosen before the time fixed for the beginning of his term, or if the President elect shall have failed to qualify, then the Vice President elect shall act as President until a President shall have qualified; and the Congress may by law provide for the case wherein neither a President elect nor a Vice President elect shall have qualified, declaring who shall then act as President, or the manner in which one who is to act shall be selected, and such person shall act accordingly until a President or Vice President shall have qualified.

4. The Congress may by law provide for the case of the death of any of the persons from whom the House of Representatives may choose a President whenever the right of choice shall have devolved upon them, and for the case of the death of any of the persons from whom the Senate may choose a Vice President whenever the right of choice shall have devolved upon them.

5. Sections 1 and 2 shall take effect on the 15th day of October following the ratification of this article.

6. This article shall be inoperative unless it shall have been ratified as an amendment to the Constitution by the legislatures of three-fourths of the several States within seven years from the date of its submission.

Amendment 21 - Amendment 18 Repealed. Ratified 12/5/1933.

1. The eighteenth article of amendment to the Constitution of the United States is hereby repealed.

2. The transportation or importation into any State, Territory, or possession of the United States for delivery or use therein of intoxicating liquors, in violation of the laws thereof, is hereby prohibited.

3. The article shall be inoperative unless it shall have been ratified as an amendment to the Constitution by conventions in the several States, as provided in the Constitution, within seven years from the date of the submission hereof to the States by the Congress.

Amendment 22 - Presidential Term Limits. Ratified 2/27/1951.

1. No person shall be elected to the office of the President more than twice, and no person who has held the office of President, or acted as President, for more than two years of a term to which some other person was elected President shall be elected to the office of the President more than once. But this Article shall not apply to any person holding the office of President, when this Article was proposed by the Congress, and shall not prevent any person who may be holding the office of President, or acting as President, during the term within which this Article becomes operative from holding the office of President or acting as President during the remainder of such term.

2. This article shall be inoperative unless it shall have been ratified as an amendment to the Constitution by the legislatures of three-fourths of the several States within seven years from the date of its submission to the States by the Congress.

Amendment 23 - Presidential Vote for District of Columbia. Ratified 3/29/1961.

1. The District constituting the seat of Government of the United States shall appoint in such manner as the Congress may direct: A number of electors of President and Vice President equal to the whole number of Senators and Representatives in Congress to which the District would be entitled if it were a State, but in no event more than the least populous State; they shall be in addition to those appointed by the States, but they shall be considered, for the purposes of the election of President and Vice President, to be electors appointed by a State; and they shall meet in the District and perform such duties as provided by the twelfth article of amendment.

2. The Congress shall have power to enforce this article by appropriate legislation.

Amendment 24 - Poll Tax Barred. Ratified 1/23/1964.

1. The right of citizens of the United States to vote in any primary or other election for President or Vice President, for electors for President or Vice President, or for Senator or

Representative in Congress, shall not be denied or abridged by the United States or any State by reason of failure to pay any poll tax or other tax.

2. The Congress shall have power to enforce this article by appropriate legislation.

Amendment 25 - Presidential Disability and Succession. Ratified 2/10/1967.

1. In case of the removal of the President from office or of his death or resignation, the Vice President shall become President.

2. Whenever there is a vacancy in the office of the Vice President, the President shall nominate a Vice President who shall take office upon confirmation by a majority vote of both Houses of Congress.

3. Whenever the President transmits to the President pro tempore of the Senate and the Speaker of the House of Representatives his written declaration that he is unable to discharge the powers and duties of his office, and until he transmits to them a written declaration to the contrary, such powers and duties shall be discharged by the Vice President as Acting President.

4. Whenever the Vice President and a majority of either the principal officers of the executive departments or of such other body as Congress may by law provide, transmit to the President pro tempore of the Senate and the Speaker of the House of Representatives their written declaration that the President is unable to discharge the powers and duties of his office, the Vice President shall immediately assume the powers and duties of the office as Acting President.

Thereafter, when the President transmits to the President pro tempore of the Senate and the Speaker of the House of Representatives his written declaration that no inability exists, he shall resume the powers and duties of his office unless the Vice President and a majority of either the principal officers of the executive department or of such other body as Congress may by law provide, transmit within four days to the President pro tempore of the Senate and the Speaker of the House of Representatives their written declaration that the President is unable to discharge the powers and duties of his office. Thereupon Congress shall decide the issue, assembling within forty eight hours for that purpose if not in session. If the Congress, within twenty one days after receipt of the latter written declaration, or, if Congress is not in session, within twenty one days after Congress is required to assemble, determines by two thirds vote of both Houses that the President is unable to discharge the powers and duties of his office, the Vice President shall continue to discharge the same as Acting President; otherwise, the President shall resume the powers and duties of his office.

Amendment 26 - Voting Age Set to 18 Years. Ratified 7/1/1971.

1. The right of citizens of the United States, who are eighteen years of age or older, to vote shall not be denied or abridged by the United States or by any State on account of age.

2. The Congress shall have power to enforce this article by appropriate legislation.

Amendment 27 - Limiting Congressional Pay Increases. Ratified 5/7/1992.

No law, varying the compensation for the services of the Senators and Representatives, shall take effect, until an election of Representatives shall have intervened.

This file was prepared by USConstitution.net. Find us on the web at http://www.usconstitution.net.

미합중국 헌법

국 가	미국
원법률명	The Constitution of the United States of America
제 정	1787.09.17
개 정	1992.05.07
수록자료	세계의 헌법 : 35개국 헌법 전문. 1, pp.466-481
발행사항	국회도서관, 2010

이 번역문은 외국 법률의 해석이나 이해를 돕기 위한 자료이며, 법적효력이 없습니다.

http://www.nanet.go.kr

미합중국 헌법[1)]

전 문

우리 합중국 국민은 좀 더 완벽한 연방을 형성하고, 정의를 확립하며, 국내의 안녕을 보장하고, 공동방위를 도모하고, 국민복지를 증진하고 우리와 우리의 후손들을 위한 자유와 축복을 확보할 목적으로 이 미합중국 헌법을 제정한다.

제1조 입법부

제1항 (입법권)

이 헌법에 의하여 부여되는 모든 입법권은 합중국의회에 속하며, 합중국의회는 상원과 하원으로 구성한다.

제2항 (하원)

1. 하원은 각 주(states)의 주민이 2년마다 선출하는 의원으로 구성하며, 각 주의 선거인은 가장 많은 의원을 가진 주의회의 선거인에게 요구되는 자격요건을 구비하여야 한다.
2. 누구든지 연령이 25세에 미달한 자, 합중국 시민으로서의 기간이 7년이 되지 아니한 자, 그리고 선거 당시에 선출되는 주의 주민이 아닌 자는 하원의원이 될 수 없다.
3. 하원의원수와 직접세는 연방에 가입하는 각 주의 인구수에 비례하여 각 주에 배정한다. 각 주의 인구수는 연기계약 노무자를 포함한 자유인의 총수에, 과세하지 아니하는 인디언을 제외하고, 그 밖의 인구총수의 5분의 3을 가산하여 결정한다. 인구수의 산정은 제1회 합중국의회를 개회한 후 3년 이내에 행하며, 그 후는 10년마다 법률이 정하는 바에 따라 행한다. 하원의원 수는 인구 3만 명당 1인의 비율을 초과하지 못한다. 다만, 각 주는 적어도 1명의 하원의원을 가져야 한다. 위의 인구수의 산정이 있을 때까지 뉴햄프셔주는 3명, 매사추세츠주는 8명, 로드아일랜드주와 프로비던스 식민지(Providence Plantations)는 1명, 코네티컷주는 5명, 뉴욕주는 6명, 뉴저지주는 4명, 펜실베이니아주는 8명, 델라웨어주는 1명, 메릴랜드주는 6명, 버지니아주는 10명, 노스 캐롤라이나주는 5명, 사우스 캐롤라이나주는 5명, 그리고 조지아주는 3명의 의원을 각각 선출할 수 있다.
4. 어느 주에서, 그 주에서 선출된 하원의원에 결원이 생겼을 경우에는 그 주의 행정부가 그 결원을 채우기 위한 보궐선거의 명령을 내려야 한다.
5. 하원은 그 의장과 그 밖의 임원을 선임하며, 탄핵권을 독점하여 가진다.

제3항 (상원)

1. 상원은 각 주의 주의회에서 선출한 6년 임기의 상원의원 2명씩으로 구성되며, 각 상원의원은 1표의 투표권을 가진다.
2. 상원의원들이 제1회 선거의 결과로 당선되어 회합하면, 즉시 의원총수를 가능한 한 동수의 3개 부류로 나눈다. 제1부류의 의원은 2년 만기로 제2부류의 의원은 4년 만기로 그리고 제3부류의 의원은 6년 만기로,

---

1) 참고문헌
 - 중앙선거관리위원회, 「미국 연방선거운동관계법」. 서울 : 중앙선거관리위원회, 2004.
 - 문홍주, 「미국헌법과 기본적 인권」. 서울 : 유풍출판사, 2002.
 - 강승식, 「미국헌법학강의」. 서울 : 궁리, 2007.

그 의석을 비워야 한다. 이렇게 하여 상원의원 총수의 3분의 1이 2년마다 개선될 수 있게 한다. 그리고 어느 주에 있어서나 주의회의 휴회 중에 사직 또는 그 밖의 원인으로 상원의원의 결원이 생길 때에는 그 주의 행정부는 다음 회기의 주의회가 결원의 보충을 할 때까지 잠정적으로 상원의원을 임명할 수 있다.

3. 연령이 30세에 미달하거나 합중국시민으로서의 기간이 9년이 되지 아니하거나 또는 선거 당시 선출되는 주의 주민이 아닌 자는 상원의원이 될 수 없다.
4. 합중국의 부통령은 상원의장이 된다. 다만, 의결시 가부 동수일 경우를 제외하고는 투표권이 없다.
5. 상원은 의장 이외의 임원들을 선임하며 부통령이 결원일 경우이거나 부통령이 대통령의 직무를 집행하는 때에는 임시의장을 선임한다.
6. 상원은 모든 탄핵에 대한 심판의 권한을 독점하여 가진다. 이 목적을 위하여 상원이 개회될 때, 의원들은 선서 또는 확약을 하여야 한다. 합중국 대통령에 대한 심판을 하는 경우에는 연방대법원장을 의장으로 한다. 누구라도 출석의원 3분의 2 이상의 찬성 없이는 유죄판결을 받지 아니한다.
7. 탄핵 결정은 면직, 그리고 합중국에서의 명예직, 위임직 또는 유급 공직에 재직하는 자격을 박탈하는 것 이상이 될 수 없다. 다만, 이같이 유죄 판결을 받은 자일지라도 법률의 규정에 따른 기소, 재판, 판결 및 처벌을 면할 수 없다.

제4항 (연방의회의 조직)

1. 상원의원과 하원의원을 선거할 시기, 장소 및 방법은 각 주에서 그 주의회가 정한다. 그러나 합중국의회는 언제든지 법률에 의하여 그러한 규정을 제정 또는 개정할 수 있다. 다만, 상원의원의 선거 장소에 관하여는 예외로 한다.
2. 연방의회는 매년 적어도 1회 집회하여야 한다. 그 집회의 시기는 법률에 의하여 다른 날짜를 지정하지 아니하는 한 12월의 첫째 월요일로 한다.

제5항 (연방의회의 운영)

1. 각 원은 그 소속 의원의 당선, 득표수 및 자격을 판정한다. 각 원은 소속 의원의 과반수가 출석함으로써 의사를 진행시킬 수 있는 정족수를 구성한다. 정족수에 미달하는 경우에는 연일 휴회할 수 있으며, 각 원에서 정하는 방법과 벌칙에 따라 결석의원의 출석을 강요할 수 있다.
2. 각 원은 의사규칙을 결정하며, 원내의 질서를 문란케 한 의원을 징계하며, 의원 3분의 2 이상의 찬성을 얻어 의원을 제명할 수 있다.
3. 각 원은 의사록을 작성하여 각 원에서 비밀에 붙여져야 한다고 판단하는 부분을 제외하고 수시로 공표하여야 한다. 각 원은 출석의원수의 5분의 1 이상이 요구할 경우에 어떠한 문제에 대해서도 소속의원의 찬반투표수를 의사록에 기재하여야 한다.
4. 연방의회의 회기 중에는 어느 원이라도 다른 원의 동의 없이 3일 이상 휴회하거나, 회의장을 양원이 개회한 장소 이외의 장소로 옮길 수 없다.

제6항 (연방의원의 특권과 겸임의 금지)

1. 상원의원과 하원의원은 그 직무에 대하여 법률이 정하고 합중국 국고로부터 지급되는 보수를 받는다. 양원의 의원은 반역죄, 중죄 및 치안 방해죄를 제외하고는 어떠한 경우에도 그 원의 회의에 출석 중에 그리고 의사당까지의 왕복 도중에 체포되지 아니하는 특권이 있다. 양원의 의원은 원내에서 행한 발언이나 토론에 관하여 원외에서 문책받지 아니한다.
2. 상원의원 또는 하원의원은 재임 기간 중에 신설되거나 봉급이 인상된 어떠한 합중국 공직에도 임명될 수 없다. 합중국의 어떠한 공직에 있는 자라도 재직 중에 양원 중 어느 원의 의원도 될 수 없다.

제7항 (법률의 제정)
1. 세입 징수에 관한 모든 법률안은 먼저 하원에서 제안되어야 한다. 다만, 상원은 이에 대해 다른 법안에서와 마찬가지로 수정안을 발의하거나 수정을 가하여 동의할 수 있다.
2. 상원과 하원을 모두 통과한 모든 법률안은 법률로 확정되기에 앞서 대통령에게 이송되어야 한다. 대통령이 이를 승인하는 경우에는 이에 서명하며, 승인하지 아니하는 경우에는 이의서를 첨부하여 이 법률안을 발의한 원으로 환부하여야 한다. 법률안을 환부받은 원은 이의의 개요를 의사록에 기록한 후 이 법률안을 다시 심의하여야 한다. 다시 심의한 결과, 그 원의 의원 3분의 2 이상의 찬성으로 가결할 경우에는 법률안을 대통령의 이의서와 함께 다른 원으로 이송하여야 한다. 다른 원에서 이 법률안을 재심의하여 의원의 3분의 2 이상의 찬성으로 가결할 경우에는 이 법률안은 법률로 확정된다. 이 모든 경우에 있어서 양원은 호명구두표결로 결정하며, 그 법률안에 대한 찬성자와 반대자의 성명을 각 원의 의사록에 기재하여야 한다. 법률안이 대통령에게 이송된 후 10일 이내 (일요일 제외)에 의회로 환부되지 아니할 때에는 그 법률안은 대통령이 이에 서명한 경우와 마찬가지의 법률로 확정된다. 다만, 연방의회가 휴회하여 이 법률안을 환부할 수 없는 경우에는 법률로 확정되지 아니한다.
3. 양원의 의결을 필요로 하는 모든 명령, 결의 또는 표결(휴회에 관한 결의는 제외)은 이를 대통령에게 이송하여야 하며, 대통령이 이를 승인하여야 효력을 발생한다. 대통령이 이를 승인하지 아니하는 경우에는 법률안에서와 같은 규칙 및 제한에 따라서 상원과 하원에서 3분의 2 이상의 의원의 찬성으로 다시 가결하여야 한다.

제8항 (연방의회에 부여된 권한)
연방의회는 다음의 권한을 가진다.
1. 합중국의 채무를 지불하고, 공동 방위와 일반 복지를 위하여 조세, 관세, 공과금 및 소비세를 부과징수한다. 다만, 관세, 공과금 및 소비세는 합중국 전역을 통하여 획일적이어야 한다.
2. 합중국의 신용으로 금전을 차입한다.
3. 외국과의, 주 상호간의 그리고 인디언부족과의 통상을 규제한다.
4. 시민권 부여에 관한 통일적인 규정과 합중국 전체를 위한 파산에 관한 통일적인 법률을 제정한다.
5. 화폐를 주조하고, 미국 화폐 및 외국 화폐의 가치를 규정하며, 도량형의 기준을 정한다.
6. 합중국의 유가증권 및 통화의 위조에 관한 벌칙을 정한다.
7. 우편관서와 우편 도로를 건설한다.
8. 저작자와 발명자에게 그들의 저술과 발명에 대한 독점적인 권리를 일정기간 확보해 줌으로써 과학과 유용한 기술의 발달을 촉진시킨다.
9. 연방대법원 아래에 하급법원을 조직한다.
10. 공해에서 발생한 해적행위와 중죄 그리고 국제법에 위배되는 범죄를 정의하고 이에 대한 벌칙을 정한다.
11. 전쟁을 포고하고, 나포인허장을 수여하고, 지상 및 해상의 포획에 관한 규칙을 정한다.
12. 육군을 모집, 편성하고 이를 유지한다. 다만, 이 목적을 위한 경비의 지출기간은 2년을 초과하지 못한다.
13. 해군을 창설하고 이를 유지한다.
14. 육해군의 통수 및 규제에 관한 규칙을 정한다.
15. 연방 법률을 집행하고, 반란을 진압하고, 침략을 격퇴하기 위하여 민병의 소집에 관한 규칙을 정한다.
16. 민병대의 편성, 무장 및 훈련에 관한 규칙과 합중국의 군무에 복무하는 자들을 다스리는 규칙을 정한다. 다만, 각 주는 민병대의 장교를 임명하고, 연방의회가 정한 군율에 따라 민병대를 훈련시키는 권한을 각각 보유한다.
17. 특정주가 합중국에게 양도하고, 연방의회가 이를 수령함으로써 합중국정부 소재지로 되는 지역(10평방마일을 초과하지 못함)에 대하여는 어떠한 경우를 막론하고 독점적인 입법권을 행사하며, 요새, 무기고, 조병창, 조선소 및 기타 필요한 건물을 세우기 위하여 주의회의 승인을 얻어 구입한 모든 장소에 대해서

도 이와 똑같은 권한을 행사한다.
   18. 위에 기술한 권한들과, 이 헌법이 합중국 정부 또는 그 부처 또는 그 관리에게 부여한 모든 기타 권한을 행사하는데 필요하고 적절한 모든 법률을 제정한다.

제9항 (연방의회에 금지된 권한)
1. 연방의회는 기존 각 주중 어느 주가 허용함이 적당하다고 인정하는 사람들의 이주 또는 입국을 1808년 이전에는 금지하지 못한다. 다만, 이러한 사람들의 입국에 대하여 1인당 10달러를 초과하지 아니하는 한도 내에서 입국세를 부과할 수 있다.
2. 인신보호영장에 관한 특권은 반란 또는 침략의 경우에 공공의 안전상 요구되는 때를 제외하고는 이를 정지시킬 수 없다.
3. 사권박탈법 또는 소급처벌법을 통과시키지 못한다.
4. 인두세나 그 밖의 직접세는 앞서(제2항제3호에) 규정한 인구조사 또는 산정에 비례하지 아니하는 한, 이를 부과하지 못한다.
5. 주로부터 수출되는 물품에 조세 또는 관세를 부과하지 못한다.
6. 어떠한 통상 또는 세수입 규정에 의하여서도 다른 주의 항구보다 특혜적인 대우를 어느 주의 항구에 할 수 없다. 또한 어느 주에 도착 예정이거나 어느 주를 출항한 선박을 다른 주에서 강제로 입·출항 수속을 하게 하거나 관세를 지불하게 할 수 없다.
7. 국고금은 법률에 따른 지출 승인에 의하여서만 지출할 수 있다. 또한 모든 공금의 수납 및 지출에 관한 정기적인 명세와 회계를 수시로 공표하여야 한다.
8. 합중국은 어떠한 귀족의 칭호도 수여하지 아니한다. 합중국에서 유급직 또는 위임에 의한 관직에 있는 자는 누구라도 연방의회의 승인 없이는 어떠한 국왕, 왕족 또는 외국으로부터도 종류 여하를 막론하고 선물, 보수, 관직 또는 칭호를 받을 수 없다.

제10항 (주에 금지된 권한)
1. 어느 주라도 조약, 동맹 또는 연합을 체결하거나, 나포면허장을 수여하거나, 화폐를 주조하거나, 신용증권을 발행하거나, 금화 및 은화 이외의 것으로서 채무지불의 법정수단으로 삼거나, 사권박탈법, 소급처벌법 또는 계약상의 의무에 해를 주는 법률 등을 제정하거나, 또는 귀족의 칭호를 수여할 수 없다.
2. 어느 주라도 연방의회의 동의 없이는 수입품 또는 수출품에 대하여 검사법의 시행 상 절대 필요한 경우를 제외하고는 공과금 또는 관세를 부과하지 못한다. 어느 주에서나 수입품 또는 수출품에 부과하는 모든 공과금이나 관세의 순수입은 합중국 재무성의 용도에 제공하여야 한다. 또한 연방의회는 이런 종류의 모든 주법들을 개정하고 통제할 수 있다.
3. 어느 주라도 연방의회의 동의 없이는 선박에 대하여 세금을 부과하거나 평화 시에 군대나 군함을 보유하거나 다른 주나 외국과 협정이나 맹약을 체결할 수 없으며, 실제로 침공당하고 있거나 지체할 수 없을 만큼 급박한 위험에 처해 있지 아니하고는 교전할 수 없다.

제2조 대통령

제1항 (대통령선거, 권한대행)
1. 행정권은 미합중국 대통령에게 속한다. 대통령의 임기는 4년으로 하며, 동일한 임기의 부통령과 함께 다음과 같은 방법에 의하여 선출된다.
2. 각 주는 그 주의회가 정하는 바에 따라, 그 주가 연방의회에 보낼 수 있는 상원의원과 하원의원의 총수와

동수의 선거인을 임명한다. 다만, 상원의원이나 하원의원 또는 합중국에서 위임에 의한 또는 유급의 관직에 있는 자는 선거인이 될 수 없다.

3. 선거인은 각기 자기 주에서 회합하여 비밀투표에 의하여 2인을 선거한다. 다만, 양인 중 적어도 1인은 선거인과 동일한 주의 주민이 아니어야 한다. 선거인은 모든 득표자들의 명부와 각 득표자의 득표수를 기재한 표를 작성하여 서명하고 증명한 다음, 봉함하여 상원의장 앞으로 합중국정부의 소재지로 송부한다. 상원의장은 상원의원 및 하원의원 앞에서 모든 증명서를 개봉하고 계산한다. 최고득표자의 득표수가 임명된 선거인의 총수의 과반수가 되었을 때에는 그가 대통령으로 당선된다. 과반수 득표자가 2인 이상이 되고, 그 득표수가 동수일 경우에는 하원이 즉시 비밀투표로 그 중 1인을 대통령으로 선임하여야 한다. 과반수 득표자가 없을 경우에는 하원이 동일한 방법으로 최다수득표자 5명중에서 대통령을 선임한다. 다만, 이러한 방법에 의하여 대통령을 선거할 때에는 선거를 주단위로 하고 각 주의 대표자는 1표의 투표권을 가지며, 그 선거에 필요한 정족수는 전체 주의 3분의 2의 주로부터 1명 또는 2명 이상의 의원의 출석으로써 성립되며, 전체 주의 과반수의 찬성을 얻어야 선출될 수 있다. 어떤 경우에 있어서나 대통령을 선출하고 난 후에 최다수의 득표를 한 자를 부통령으로 한다. 다만, 동수의 득표자가 2인 이상 있을 때에는 상원이 비밀투표로 그 중에서 부통령을 선출한다.

4. 연방의회는 선거인들의 선임시기와 이들의 투표일을 결정할 수 있으며, 이 투표일은 합중국 전역을 통하여 같은 날이 되어야 한다.

5. 출생에 의한 합중국시민이 아닌 자, 또는 본 헌법의 제정 시에 합중국 시민이 아닌 자는 대통령으로 선임될 자격이 없다. 연령이 35세에 미달한 자, 또는 14년간 합중국 내의 주민이 아닌 자도 대통령으로 선임될 자격이 없다.

6. 대통령이 면직되거나, 사망하거나, 사직하거나 또는 그 권한 및 직무를 수행할 능력을 상실할 경우에 대통령의 직무는 부통령에게 귀속된다. 연방의회는 법률에 의하여 대통령 및 부통령의 면직 또는 직무수행 불능의 경우를 규정할 수 있으며, 그러한 경우에 대통령의 직무를 수행할 관리를 정할 수 있다. 이 관리는 대통령의 직무수행 불능이 제거되거나 대통령이 새로 선임될 때까지 대통령의 직무를 대행한다.

7. 대통령은 그 직무수행에 대한 대가로 정기적으로 보수를 받으며, 그 보수는 임기 중에 인상 또는 인하되지 아니한다. 대통령은 그 임기 중에 합중국 또는 어느 주로부터 그 밖의 어떠한 보수도 받지 못한다.

8. 대통령은 그 직무수행을 시작하기에 앞서 다음과 같은 선서 또는 확약을 하여야 한다. "나는 합중국 대통령의 직무를 성실히 수행하며, 나의 능력의 최선을 다하여 합중국 헌법을 보전하고, 보호하고, 수호할 것을 엄숙히 선서(또는 확약)한다."

제2항 (대통령의 권한)

1. 대통령은 합중국 육해군의 총사령관 그리고 각주의 민병이 합중국의 현역에 소집되었을 때는 그 민병대의 총사령관이 된다. 대통령은 행정 각 부의 장관에게 소관 직무사항에 관하여 문서에 의한 견해를 요구할 수 있다. 대통령은 합중국에 대한 범죄에 관하여 탄핵의 경우를 제외하고, 형의 집행유예 및 사면을 명할 수 있는 권한을 가진다.

2. 대통령은 상원의 권고와 동의를 얻어 조약을 체결하는 권한을 가진다. 다만, 그 권고와 동의는 상원의 출석의원 3분의 2 이상의 찬성을 얻어야 한다. 대통령은 대사, 그 밖의 공사 및 영사, 연방대법원 판사, 그리고 그 임명에 관하여 본 헌법에 특별 규정이 없고 법률로써 정하는 그 밖의 모든 합중국 관리를 지명하여 상원의 권고와 동의를 얻어 임명한다. 다만, 연방의회는 적당하다고 인정되는 하급관리 임명권을 법률에 의하여 대통령에게, 법원에게, 또는 각부장관에게 부여할 수 있다.

3. 대통령은 상원의 휴회 중에 생기는 모든 결원을 임명에 의하여 충원하는 권한을 가진다. 다만, 그 임명은 다음 회기가 만료될 때에 효력을 상실한다.

제3항 (보고 및 의회의 소집)

대통령은 연방의 상황에 관하여 수시로 연방의회에 보고하고, 필요하고 권고할 만하다고 인정하는 법안의 심의를 연방의회에 권고하여야 한다. 긴급 시에 대통령은 상·하 양원 또는 그 중의 1원을 소집할 수 있으며, 휴회의 시기에 관하여 양원간에 의견이 일치되지 아니하는 때에는 대통령은 적당하다고 인정하는 때까지 양원의 정회를 명할 수 있다. 대통령은 대사와 그 밖의 외교사절을 접수하며, 법률이 충실하게 집행되도록 유의하며, 또 합중국의 모든 관리들에게 직무를 위임한다.

제4항 (탄핵)

대통령, 부통령 그리고 합중국의 모든 문관은 반역죄, 수뢰죄, 또는 그 밖의 중대한 범죄 등으로 탄핵을 받거나 유죄 판결을 받는 경우 그 직에서 면직된다.

제3조 사법부

제1항 (법원)

합중국의 사법권은 1개의 연방대법원에, 그리고 연방의회가 수시로 제정 설치하는 하급법원들에 속한다. 연방대법원 및 하급법원의 판사는 중대한 죄가 없는 한 그 직을 보유하며, 그 직무에 대하여 정기에 보수를 받으며, 그 보수는 재임 중에 감액되지 아니한다.

제2항 (재판의 관할)

1. 사법권은 본 헌법과 합중국 법률과 그리고 합중국의 권한에 의하여 체결되었거나 체결될 조약으로 인하여 발생하는 모든 보통법상 및 형평법상의 사건, 대사와 그 밖의 외교사절 및 영사에 관한 모든 사건, 해사재판 및 해상관할에 관한 모든 사건, 합중국이 한 편의 당사자가 되는 쟁송, 2개 주 또는 그 이상의 주간에 발생하는 쟁송, 한 주와 타 주시민 간의 쟁송, 상이한 주의 시민 사이의 쟁송, 다른 주로부터 부여받은 토지의 권리에 관하여 같은 주의 시민 사이에 발생하는 쟁송 및 1개 주 또는 그 주민과 외국 또는 그 시민 또는 그 시민 간에 발생하는 쟁송에 미친다.
2. 대사와 그 밖의 외교사절 및 영사에 관계되는 사건과 주가 당사자인 사건은 연방대법원이 제1심의 재판관할권을 가진다. 그 밖의 모든 사건에 있어서는 연방의회가 정하는 예외의 경우를 두되, 연방의회가 정하는 규정에 따라 법률문제와 사실문제에 관하여 상소심의 재판관할권을 가진다.
3. 탄핵사건을 제외한 모든 범죄의 재판은 배심제로 한다. 그 재판은 그 범죄가 행하여진 주에서 하여야 한다. 다만, 그 범죄지가 어느 주에도 속하지 아니할 경우에는 연방의회가 법률에 의하여 정하는 장소에서 재판한다.

제3항 (반역죄)

1. 합중국에 대한 반역죄는 합중국에 대하여 전쟁을 일으키거나, 또는 적에게 가담하여 원조 및 지원을 할 경우에만 성립한다. 누구라도 명백한 상기행동에 대하여 2명의 증인의 증언이 있거나 또는 공개법정에서 자백하는 경우 이외에는 반역죄의 유죄선고를 받지 아니한다.
2. 연방의회는 반역죄의 형벌을 선고하는 권한을 가진다. 다만, 반역죄의 선고로 사권이 박탈된 자는 자기의 생존기간을 제외하고 그 혈통을 모독하거나, 상속금지나 재산 몰수를 초래하지 아니한다.

제4조 주 상호간의 관계

제1항 (신뢰)
각 주는 다른 주의 법령, 기록 및 사법절차에 대하여 충분한 신뢰와 신용을 가져야 한다. 연방의회는 이러한 법령, 기록 및 사법절차를 증명하는 방법과 그것들의 효력을 일반 법률로써 규정할 수 있다.

제2항 (특권과 면책)
1. 각 주의 시민은 다른 어느 주에서도 그 주의 시민이 향유하는 모든 특권 및 면책권을 가진다.
2. 어느 주에서 반역죄, 중죄 또는 그 밖의 범죄로 인하여 고발된 자가 도피하여 재판을 면하고 다른 주에서 발견된 경우, 범인이 도피해 나온 주의 행정당국의 요구에 의하여 그 범인은 그 범죄에 대한 재판관할권이 있는 주로 인도되어야 한다.
3. 어느 주에서 그 주의 법률에 의하여 사역 또는 노역을 당하도록 되어 있는 자가 다른 주로 도피한 경우, 다른 주의 어떠한 법률 또는 규정에 의하여서도 그 사역 또는 노역의 의무는 해제되지 아니하며, 그 자는 그 사역 또는 노역을 요구할 권리를 가진 당사자의 청구에 따라 인도되어야 한다.

제3항 (연방과 주간의 관계)
1. 연방의회는 새로운 주를 연방에 가입시킬 수 있다. 다만, 어떠한 주의 관할구역에서도 새로운 주를 형성하거나 설치할 수 없다. 또 관계 각 주의 주 의회와 연방의회의 동의 없이는 2개 이상 주 또는 주의 일부를 합병하여 신주를 형성할 수 없다.
2. 연방의회는 합중국 속령 또는 합중국에 속하는 그 밖의 재산을 처분하고 이에 관한 모든 필요한 규칙 및 규정을 제정하는 권한을 가진다. 다만, 이 헌법의 어떠한 조항도 합중국 또는 어느 주의 권리를 훼손하는 것으로 해석하여서는 안된다.

제4항 (연방의 보호)
합중국은 이 연방내의 모든 주에 공화정체를 보장하며, 각 주를 침략으로부터 보호하며, 또 각 주의 주 의회 또는 행정부(주 의회를 소집할 수 없을 때)의 요구가 있을 때에는 주 내의 폭동으로부터 각 주를 보호한다.

제5조 헌법수정 절차

연방의회는 양원 의원의 3분의 2가 본 헌법에 대한 수정의 필요성을 인정할 때에는 헌법수정을 발의하여야 한다. 또는 주 중 3분의 2 이상의 주 의회의 요청이 있을 때에는 수정발의를 위한 헌법회의를 소집하여야 한다. 어느 경우에 있어서나 수정은 연방의회가 제의한 비준의 두 방법 중의 어느 하나에 따라 4분의 3의 주의 주 의회에 의하여 비준되거나, 또는 4분의 3의 주의 주 헌법회의에 의하여 비준되는 때에는 사실상 본 헌법의 일부로서 효력을 발생한다. 다만, 1808년 이전에 이루어지는 수정은 어떠한 방법으로도 제1조제9항제1호 및 제4호에 변경을 가져올 수 없다. 어느 주도 그 주의 동의 없이는 상원에서의 동등한 투표권을 박탈당하지 아니한다.

제6조 헌법의 법적 지위

제1항 (채무와 조약)
본 헌법이 제정되기 전에 계약된 모든 채무와 체결된 모든 계약은 본 헌법 하에서도 연합규약 하에서와 마찬가지로 합중국에 대하여 효력을 가진다.

제2항 (연방의 최고성)

본 헌법 의거하여 제정되는 합중국 법률 그리고 합중국의 권한에 의하여 체결되었거나 체결될 모든 조약은 이 국가의 최고 법률이다. 모든 주의 법관은 여기에 구속되며, 1주의 헌법이나 법률 중에 이에 배치되는 규정이 있을지라도 그것에 구속되지 아니한다.

제3항

앞에서 언급한 상원의원 및 하원의원, 각 주의 의회의원, 합중국 및 각 주의 모든 행정관 및 사법관은 선서 또는 확약에 의하여 본 헌법에 충성할 의무가 있다. 다만, 종교상의 자격은 합중국의 어떠한 관직 또는 위임에 의한 공직에도 그 자격요건으로 요구되지 아니한다.

제7조 헌법 비준

본 헌법이 이를 비준하는 각 주간에 확정되기 위해서는 9개주의 주 헌법회의에 의한 비준을 필요로 한다.
서기 1787년, 미합중국 독립 제12년 9월 17일 헌법회의에서 참석한 각 주의 만장일치의 동의를 얻어 본 헌법을 제정한다. 이를 증명하기 위하여 우리들은 여기에 서명한다.

의장 겸 버지니아주 대표 : 조지 워싱턴
뉴햄프셔주 : 존 랭턴, 니콜라스 길먼
매사추세츠주 : 너대니얼 고램, 루퍼스 킹
코네티커트주 : 윌리엄 새뮤얼 존슨, 로저 셔먼
뉴욕주 : 알렉산더 해밀턴
뉴저지주 : 윌리엄 리빙스턴, 데이비드 브리얼리, 윌리엄 패터슨, 조내던 데이튼
펜실베이니아주 : 벤저민 프랭클린, 토머스 미플린, 로버트 모리스, 조지클라이머, 토머스 피치먼즈, 자레드 잉거솔, 제임스 윌슨, 구부누어 모리스
델라웨어주 : 조지 리드, 거닝 베드포드 주니어, 존 디킨슨, 리처드 배시트 제이컵 브룸
메릴랜드주 : 제임스 멕헨리, 대니얼 오브 세인트, 토머스 제니퍼, 대니얼 캐럴
버지니아주 : 존 블레어, 제임스 매디슨 주니어
노스 캐롤라이나주 : 윌리엄 블라운트, 리처드 도브스 스페이트, 휴 윌러엄슨
사우스 캐롤라이나주 : 존 러틀리지, 찰즈 코우츠워스 핑크니, 찰즈 핑크니, 피어스 버틀러
조지아주 : 윌리엄 퓨, 에이브러햄 볼드윈
인증서기 : 윌리엄 잭슨

헌법 수정 조항

아래는 미국헌법의 수정조항이다. 수정헌법의 첫 10개 조항은 권리장전이라고 알려져 있다(이 수정조항들은 1789년 9월 25일 발의되어 1791년 12월 15일에 비준됨).

수정헌법 제1조 (종교, 언론, 출판, 집회의 자유 및 청원의 권리)
연방의회는 국교를 정하거나 또는 자유로운 신앙행위를 금지하는 법률을 제정할 수 없다. 또한 언론, 출판의 자유나 국민이 평화로이 집회할 권리 및 고충의 구제를 위하여 정부에게 청원할 수 있는 국민의 권리를 제한하는 법률을 제정할 수 없다.

수정헌법 제2조 (무기소지의 권리)
기강이 확립된 민병들로서 자유로운 주의 안보에 필요한 무기를 소장하고 휴대하는 국민의 권리는 침해당하지 않는다.

수정헌법 제3조 (군인의 주둔)
평화 시에 군대는 어떠한 주택에도 그 소유자의 승낙을 받지 아니하고는 주둔할 수 없다. 전시에 있어서도 법률이 정하는 방법에 의하지 아니하고는 주둔할 수 없다.

수정헌법 제4조 (수색 및 체포영장)
부당한 수색, 체포, 압수로부터 신체, 가택, 서류 및 동산의 안전을 보장받는 국민의 권리를 침해할 수 없다. 체포, 수색, 압수의 영장은 상당한 이유에 근거하고, 선서 또는 확약에 의하여 확인되고, 특히 수색 장소, 체포될 사람 또는 압수될 물품을 기재하지 아니하고는 발급되지 아니한다.

수정헌법 제5조 (형사사건에서의 제권리)
누구라도 배심원에 의한 고발 또는 기소가 있지 아니하는 한 사형에 해당하는 죄 또는 중죄에 관하여 심리받기 위하여 구금되지 아니한다. 다만, 육군이나 해군에서 또는 전시나 사변 시에 복무 중에 있는 민병대에서 발생한 사건에 관하여서는 예외로 한다. 누구라도 동일한 범행으로 생명이나 신체에 대한 위협을 재차 받지 아니하며, 어떠한 형사 사건에 있어서도 자기에게 불리한 증언을 강요당하지 아니하며, 누구라도 정당한 법의 절차에 의하지 아니하고는 생명, 자유 또는 재산을 박탈당하지 아니한다. 또 정당한 보상 없이 사유재산을 공공용(公共用)으로 수용당하지 아니한다.

수정헌법 제6조 (공정한 재판을 받을 제권리)
모든 형사소추에 있어서, 피고인은 범죄가 행하여진 주 및 법률이 미리 정하는 지역의 공정한 배심에 의한 신속한 공판을 받을 권리, 사건의 성질과 이유에 관하여 통고 받을 권리, 자기에게 불리한 증인과 대질심문 받을 권리, 자기에게 유리한 증인을 얻기 위하여 강제적 수속을 취할 권리, 자신의 변호를 위하여 변호인의 도움을 받을 권리를 가진다.

수정헌법 제7조 (민사사건에서의 제권리)
보통법상의 소송에 있어서, 쟁송의 액수가 20달러를 초과하는 경우에는 배심에 의하여 심리를 받을 권리가 보유된다. 배심에 의하여 심리된 사실은 보통법의 규정에 의하는 이외에 합중국의 어느 법원에서도 재심 받지 아니한다.

수정헌법 제8조 (보석금, 벌금 및 형벌)
과다한 보석금을 요구하거나, 과다한 벌금을 과하거나, 잔혹하고 비정상적인 형벌을 과하지 못한다.

수정헌법 제9조 (국민이 보유하는 제권리)
본 헌법에 특정 권리들을 열거한 사실이 국민이 보유하는 그 밖의 여러 권리들을 부인하거나 경시하는 것으로 해석되어서는 아니된다.

수정헌법 제10조 (주와 국민이 보유하는 권한)
본 헌법에 의하여 연방에 위임되지 아니하였거나, 각 주에 금지되지 아니한 권한은 각 주나 국민이 보유한다.

수정헌법 제11조 (주를 상대로 하는 소송)[2]
합중국의 사법권은 합중국의 한 주에 대하여 다른 주의 시민 또는 외국의 시민이나 신민에 의하여 개시되었거나 제기된 보통법상 또는 형평법상의 소송에까지 미치는 것으로 해석할 수 없다.

수정헌법 제12조 (대통령 및 부통령의 선출)[3]
선거인은 각각 자신의 주에서 회합하여, 비밀투표에 의하여 대통령과 부통령을 선거한다. 양자 중 적어도 1인은 선거인과 동일한 주의 주민이 아니어야 한다. 선거인은 투표용지에 대통령으로 투표되는 사람의 이름을 지정하고, 별개의 투표용지에 부통령으로 투표되는 사람의 이름을 지정하여야 한다. 선거인은 대통령으로 투표된 모든 사람의 명부와 부통령으로 투표된 모든 사람의 명부 그리고 각 득표자의 득표수를 기재한 표를 별개로 작성하여 선거인이 이에 서명하고 증명한 다음 봉합하여 상원의장 앞으로 합중국 정부 소재지로 송부한다. 상원의장은 상원의원 및 하원의원 참석 하에 모든 증명서를 개봉하고 개표한다. 대통령으로서의 투표의 최고득표자를 대통령으로 한다. 다만, 득표수가 선임된 선거인의 총수의 과반수가 되어야 한다. 이와 같은 과반수 득표자가 없을 경우 하원은 즉시 대통령으로 투표된 사람의 명부 중 3인을 초과하지 아니하는 최다수 득표자들 중에서 대통령을 비밀투표로 선거하여야 한다. 다만, 이러한 방법으로 대통령을 선거할 때에는 선거를 주단위로 하고, 각 주는 1표의 투표권을 가지며, 그 선거에 필요한 정족수는 전체주의 3분의 2의 주로부터 1명 또는 그 이상의 의원의 출석으로써 성립되며, 전체 주의 과반수의 찬성을 얻어야 선출될 수 있다. 대통령선정권이 하원에 귀속된 경우에 하원이 (다음 3월 4일까지) 대통령을 선정하지 않을 때에는 대통령의 사망 또는 그 밖의 헌법상의 직무 수행 불능의 경우와 같이 부통령이 대통령의 직무를 행한다. 부통령으로서의 최고득표자를 부통령으로 한다. 다만, 그 득표수는 선임된 선거인의 총수의 과반수가 되어야 한다. 과반수 득표자가 없을 경우에는 상원이 득표자 명부 중 최다수 득표자 2인 중에서 부통령을 선임한다. 이 목적을 위한 정족수는 상원의원 총수의 3분의 2로 성립되며, 그 선임에는 의원총수의 과반수가 필요하다. 다만, 헌법상 대통령의 직에 취임할 자격이 없는 사람은 합중국 부통령의 직에 취임할 자격도 없다.

수정헌법 제13조 (노예제도 폐지)[4]

제1항
노예제도 또는 강제노역제도는 당사자가 정당하게 유죄판결을 받은 범죄에 대한 처벌이 아니면 합중국 또는 그 관할에 속하는 어느 장소에서도 인정되지 않는다.

제2항
연방의회는 적절한 입법에 의하여 본 조의 규정을 시행할 권한을 가진다.

---

[2] 이 수정조항은 1974년 3월 4일에 발의되어, 1975년 2월 7일에 비준됨.
[3] 이 수정조항은 1803년 12월 9일에 발의되어, 1804년 7월 27일에 비준됨.
[4] 이 수정조항은 1865년 1월 31일에 발의되어, 1865년 12월 6일에 비준됨.

수정헌법 제14조 (공민권)

제1항
합중국에서 출생하거나 귀화한 합중국의 관할권에 속하는 모든 사람은 합중국 및 그 거주하는 주의 시민이다. 어떠한 주도 합중국 시민의 특권과 면책권을 박탈하는 법률을 제정하거나 시행할 수 없다. 어떠한 주도 정당한 법의 절차에 의하지 아니하고는 어떠한 사람으로부터도 생명, 자유 또는 재산을 박탈할 수 없으며, 그 관할권 내에 있는 어떠한 사람에 대하여도 법률에 의한 평등한 보호를 거부하지 못한다.

제2항
하원의원은 각 주의 인구수에 비례하여 각 주에 할당한다. 인구수는 과세되지 아니하는 인디언을 제외한 수이다. 다만, 합중국 대통령 및 부통령의 선거인, 연방의회의 하원의원, 각 주의 행정관, 사법관 또는 각 주의 의회의원을 선출하는 어떠한 선거에서도 반란이나 그 밖의 범죄에 가담한 경우를 제외하고, 21세에 달하고 합중국 시민인 당해 주의 남성주민 중의 어느 누구에게 투표권이 거부되거나 어떠한 방법으로 제한되어 있을 때에는 그 주의 하원의원 할당수의 기준은 그러한 남성주민의 수가 그 주의 21세에 달한 남성주민의 총수에 대하여 가지는 비율에 따라 감소된다.

제3항
과거에 연방의회 의원, 합중국 관리, 주 의회의원 또는 각 주의 행정관이나 사법관으로서 합중국 헌법을 수호할 것을 선서하고, 후에 이에 대한 폭동이나 반란에 가담하거나 또는 그 적에게 원조를 제공한 자는 누구라도 연방의회의 상원의원이나 하원의원, 대통령 및 부통령의 선거인, 합중국이나 각 주에서 문무의 관직에 취임할 수 없다. 다만, 연방의회는 각원의 3분의 2의 찬성투표로써 그 실격을 해제할 수 있다.

제4항
폭동이나 반란을 진압할 때의 공헌에 대한 은급 및 하사금을 지불하기 위하여 발생한 부채를 포함하여 법률로 인정한 국채의 법적효력은 이를 문제로 삼을 수 없다. 그러나 합중국 또는 주는 합중국에 대한 폭동이나 반란을 원조하기 위하여 발생한 부채에 대하여 또는 노예의 상실이나 해방으로 인한 청구에 대하여서는 채무를 부담하거나 지불하지 아니한다. 모든 그러한 부채, 채무 및 청구는 위법이고 무효이다.

제5항[5]
연방의회는 적절한 입법에 의하여 본 조의 규정을 시행할 권한을 가진다.

수정헌법 제15조 (투표권의 보장)[6]

제1항
합중국 시민의 투표권은 인종, 피부색 또는 과거의 예속 상태로 인해서 합중국이나 주에 의하여 거부되거나 제한되지 아니한다.

제2항
연방의회는 적절한 입법에 의하여 본 조의 규정을 시행할 권한을 가진다.

---

[5] 이 수정조항은 1866년 6월 13일에 발의되어, 1868년 7월 9일에 비준됨.
[6] 이 수정조항은 1869년 2월 26일에 발의되어, 1870년 2월 3일에 비준됨.

수정헌법 제16조 (소득세)[7]

연방의회는 각 주에 소득세를 배당하지 아니하고 국세조사나 인구수 산정에 관계없이, 어떠한 소득원에서 얻어지는 소득에 대하여서도 소득세를 부과, 징수할 권한을 가진다.

수정헌법 제17조 (연방의회 상원의원 직접선거)[8]

제1항

합중국의 상원은 각 주에 2명씩의 상원의원으로 구성된다. 상원의원은 그 주의 주민에 의하여 선출되고 6년의 임기를 가진다. 각 상원의원은 1표의 투표권을 가진다. 각 주의 선거인은 가장 많은 의원수를 가진 주 의회의 선거인에게 요구되는 자격을 가져야 한다.

제2항

상원에서 어느 주의 의원에 결원이 생긴 때에는 그 주의 행정부는 결원을 보충하기 위하여 선거명령을 발하여야 한다. 다만, 주민이 주 의회가 정하는 선거에 의하여 결원을 보충할 때까지, 주 의회는 그 주의 행정부에 임시로 상원의원을 임명하는 권한을 부여할 수 있다.

제3항

본 수정조항은 본 헌법의 일부로서 효력을 발생하기 이전에 선출된 상원의원의 선거 또는 임기에 영향을 주는 것으로 해석하지 못한다.

수정헌법 제18조 (양조의 금지)[9]

제1항

본 조의 비준으로부터 1년을 경과한 후에는 합중국내와 그 관할에 속하는 모든 영역 내에서 음용할 목적으로 주류를 양조, 판매 또는 운송하거나 합중국에서 이를 수입 또는 수출하는 것을 금지한다.

제2항

연방의회와 각 주는 적절한 입법에 의하여 본 조를 시행할 동등할 권한을 가진다.

제3항

본 조는 연방의회로부터 이를 각 주에 회부한 날로부터 7년 이내에 각 주 의회가 헌법에 규정된 바와 같이 헌법수정으로서 비준하지 아니하면 그 효력을 발생하지 아니한다.

수정헌법 제19조 (여성의 선거권)[10]

제1항

합중국 시민의 투표권은 성별을 이유로 합중국이나 주에 의하여 거부 또는 제한되지 아니한다.

---

[7] 이 수정조항은 1909년 7월 12일에 발의되어, 1913년 2월 3일에 비준됨.
[8] 이 수정조항은 1912년 5월 13일에 발의되어, 1913년 4월 8일에 비준됨.
[9] 이 수정조항은 1917년 12월 18일에 발의되어, 1919년 1월 26일에 비준됨.
[10] 이 수정조항은 1919년 6월 4일에 발의되어, 1920년 8월 18일에 비준됨.

제2항
연방의회는 적절한 입법에 의하여 본 조를 시행할 권한을 가진다.

수정헌법 제20조 (대통령과 연방의회의원의 임기)[11]

제1항
대통령과 부통령의 임기는 본 조가 비준되지 아니하였더라면 임기가 만료하였을 해의 1월 20일 정오에 끝난다. 그리고 상원의원과 하원의원의 임기는 그 해의 1월 3일 정오에 끝난다. 그 후임자의 임기는 그때부터 시작된다.

제2항
연방의회는 매년 적어도 1회 집회한다. 그 집회는 의회가 법률로 다른 날을 정하지 아니하는 한 1월 3일 정오부터 시작된다.

제3항
대통령의 임기 개시일로 정해놓은 시일에 대통령 당선자가 사망하였으면 부통령 당선자가 대통령이 된다. 대통령 임기의 개시일로 정한 시일까지 대통령이 선정되지 아니하였거나, 대통령 당선자가 자격을 구비하지 못하였을 때에는 부통령 당선자가 대통령이 그 자격을 구비할 때까지 대통령의 직무를 대행한다. 연방의회는 대통령 당선자와 부통령 당선자가 다 자격을 구비하지 못하는 경우에 대비하여 대통령의 직무를 대행하여야 할 자 또는 그 대행자의 선정방법을 정하여 법률로써 규정하여야 한다. 이러한 경우에 선임된 자는 대통령 또는 부통령이 자격을 구비할 때까지 대통령의 직무를 대행한다.

제4항
연방의회는 하원이 대통령의 선출권을 갖게 되었을 때에 대통령으로 선출할 인사 중 사망자가 생긴 경우와 상원이 부통령의 선출권을 갖게 되었을 때에 부통령으로 선출할 인사 중 사망자가 생긴 경우를 대비하여 법률로 규정할 수 있다.

제5항
제1항 및 제2항은 본 조의 비준 후 최초의 10월 15일부터 효력을 발생한다.

제6항
본 조는 회부된 날로부터 7년 이내에 각 주의 4분의 3의 주 의회에 의하여 헌법수정 조항으로 비준되지 아니하면 효력을 발생하지 아니한다.

수정헌법 제21조 (금주조항의 폐기)[12]

제1항
연방 수정헌법 제18조를 폐기한다.

제2항
합중국의 주 영토 또는 속령의 법률을 위반하여 이들 지역 내에서 주류를 운송 또는 사용할 목적으로 수송

---
11) 이 수정조항은 1932년 3월 2일에 발의되어, 1933년 1월 23일에 비준됨.
12) 이 수정조항은 1933년 2월 20일에 발의되어, 1933년 12월 5일에 비준됨.

또는 수입하는 것을 금지한다.

제3항

본 조는 연방의회가 이것을 각 주에게 발의한 날부터 7년 이내에 헌법규정에 따라서 각 주의 헌법회의에 의하여 헌법수정조항으로서 비준되지 아니하면 효력을 발생하지 아니한다.

수정헌법 제22조 (대통령임기를 2회로 제한)[13]

제1항

누구라도 2회를 초과하여 대통령직에 선출될 수 없으며, 타인이 대통령으로 당선된 임기 중 2년 이상 대통령직에 있었거나 대통령 직무를 대행한 자는 1회를 초과하여 대통령직에 당선될 수 없다. 다만, 본 조는 연방의회가 이를 발의하였을 때에 대통령직에 있는 자에게는 적용되지 아니하며, 또 본조가 효력을 발생하게 될 때에 대통령직에 있거나 대통령 직무를 대행하고 있는 자가 잔여임기 중 대통령직에 있거나 대통령 직무를 대행하는 것을 방해하지 아니한다.

제2항

본 조는 연방의회가 각 주에 회부한 날로부터 7년 이내에 각 주의 4분의 3의 주 의회에 의하여 헌법수정조항으로서 비준되지 아니하면 효력을 발생하지 아니한다.

수정헌법 제23조 (콜럼비아 특별행정구에서의 선거권)[14]

제1항

합중국 정부소재지를 구성하고 있는 지구는 연방의회가 다음과 같이 정한 방식에 따라 대통령 및 부통령의 선거인을 임명한다.

그 선거인의 수는 이 지구가 하나의 주라면 배당받을 수 있는 연방의원내의 상원 및 하원 의원수와 동일한 수이다. 그러나 어떠한 경우에도 최소의 인구를 가진 주보다 더 많을 수 없다. 그들은 각 주가 임명한 선거인들에 첨가된다. 그러나 그들도 대통령 및 부통령의 선거를 위하여 주가 선정한 선거인으로 간주된다. 그들은 이 지구에서 회합하여 헌법수정조항 제12조가 규정하고 있는 바와 같은 직무를 수행한다.

제2항

합중국 의회는 적절한 입법에 의하여 본 조를 시행할 권한을 가진다.

수정헌법 제24조 (투표세)[15]

제1항

대통령 또는 부통령 선거인들 또는 합중국의회 상원의원이나 하원의원을 위한 예비선거 또는 그 밖의 선거에서의 합중국 시민의 선거권은 인두세나 기타 조세를 납부하지 아니하였다는 이유로 합중국 또는 주에 의하여 거부되거나 제한되지 아니한다.

---

[13] 이 수정조항은 1947년 3월 24일에 발의되어, 1951년 2월 27일에 비준됨.
[14] 이 수정조항은 1960년 6월 16일에 발의되어, 1961년 3월 29일에 비준됨.
[15] 이 수정조항은 1962년 8월 27일에 발의되어, 1964년 1월 23일에 비준됨.

제2항

합중국 의회는 적절한 입법에 의하여 본 조를 시행할 권한을 가진다.

수정헌법 제25조 (대통령의 직무수행불능과 승계)[16]

제1항

대통령이 면직, 사망 또는 사임하는 경우에는 부통령이 대통령이 된다.

제2항

부통령직이 궐위되었을 때에는 대통령이 부통령을 지명하고, 그는 양원의 과반수득표에 의하여 승인을 얻어 그 직에 취임한다.

제3항

대통령이 상원의 임시의장과 하원의장에게 대통령의 권한과 임무를 수행할 수 없다는 것을 기재한 공한을 송부할 경우에는 이와 반대되는 서면성명서가 나올 때까지 대통령권한대행으로서 그 권한과 임무를 수행한다.

제4항

부통령과 연방의회가 법률이 정하는 행정부 주요 공무원 또는 기타 기관의 장들의 대다수가 상원의 임시의장과 하원의장에게 대통령이 그의 권한과 임무를 수행할 수 없다는 것을 기재한 공한을 송부할 경우에는 부통령이 즉시 대통령권한대행으로서 대통령직의 권한과 임무를 수행한다.

그리고 대통령이 상원의 임시의장과 하원의장에게 직무수행 불능이 존재하지 아니하다는 것을 기재한 공한을 송부할 때는 대통령이 그의 권한과 임무를 다시 수행한다. 다만, 그러한 경우에 부통령, 행정부 또는 연방의회가 법률에 의하여 규정하는 기타 기관의 장들의 대다수가 4일 이내에 상원의 임시의장과 하원의장에게 대통령이 그의 권한과 임무를 수행할 수 없다는 것을 기재한 서면설명서를 송부하는 경우에는 예외로 한다. 그 경우에 연방의회는 비회기중이라 할지라도 목적을 위하여 48시간 이내에 소집하여 그 문제를 결정한다. 연방의회가 후자의 공한을 수령한 후 21일 이내에 또는 비회기중이라도 연방의회가 소집 요구를 받은 후 21일 이내에 양원의 3분의 2의 표결로써 대통령이 그의 직무의 권한과 임무를 수행할 수 없다는 것을 결의할 경우에는 부통령이 대통령권한대행으로서 계속하여 그 권한과 임무를 수행한다. 다만, 그렇지 아니한 경우에는 대통령이 그의 권한과 임무를 다시 수행한다.

수정헌법 제26조 (18세 이상인 시민의 선거권)[17]

제1항

연령 18세 이상의 합중국 시민의 투표권은 연령을 이유로 하여 합중국 또는 주에 의하여 거부되거나 제한되지 아니한다.

제2항

합중국 의회는 적절한 입법에 의하여 본 조를 시행할 권한을 가진다.

---

16) 이 수정조항은 1965년 7월 6일에 발의되어, 1967년 2월 10일에 비준됨.
17) 이 수정조항은 1971년 3월 23일에 발의되어, 1971년 7월 1일에 비준됨.

수정헌법 제27조 (의원 세비 인상)[18]
 상·하의원의 세비변경에 관한 법률은 다음 하원의원 선거 때까지 효력을 발생하지 않는다.

---

18) 이 수정조항은 1992년 5월 7일에 비준됨.